Stories From
INNER
space
Confessions
Of A Preacher Woman and Other Tales

Praise For

Stories from INNER SPACE:
Confessions of A Preacher Woman and Other Tales

"Claudette Anderson Copeland has secured her place in history as one of the premier preachers of the twenty-first century. Her proclamation from sacred desks around the world has encouraged and challenged hearers to drink deeply from the well of the Gospel, by being doers and not just hearers only. In this book she provides definite examples of the wisdom needed to navigate the sometimes perilous waters of ministry, and life.

These stories are reflective, gritty and honest.

They give us reason to pause, to pray and to give praise.

We are all deeply indebted to this preacher for providing us a glimpse of how one traverses the journey with faith, fortitude and grace. Thanks be to God for this faithful servant who offers us a fresh word!"

The Reverend Martha Simmons, Esquire. Co-Executive Editor of the African American Pulpit Journal and 9.11.01 African American Leaders Respond to an American Tragedy. Editor, Preaching On the Brink, Boston, MA.

*

"The things that breed competence and clarity in ministry are not always learned in academic circles alone. More often, they are lived, and discovered again and again at the 'bottom of the well.' Dr. Copeland's book, Stories from INNER SPACE: Confessions of a Preacher Woman, reminds us of the hidden ingredients that make beautiful women strong, and strong women beautiful. It will hold you till the very last page!"

The Bishop Kenneth Ulmer. D. Min., Ph.D., Author, educator; Senior Pastor, Faithful Central Bible Church, Inglewood, CA.

Stories From
INNER
space

Confessions
Of A Preacher Woman and Other Tales

Also By Claudette Anderson Copeland

Coming Through the Darkness:

Cancer and One Woman's Journey to Wholeness

(2000)

And

Coming Through:

A Companion Journal and Guide to Prayer

For Specific Woman Seasons

(2000)

Stories From
INNER
space

Confessions
Of A Preacher Woman and Other Tales

Claudette Anderson Copeland

RED NAIL PRESS

A Subsidiary of Destiny Press of San Antonio
San Antonio, Texas

1st Printing
© Copyright 2003

Library of Congress Card Number Pending

ISBN 0-9700977-1-9

RED NAIL PRESS

Cover Design by Shokare Nakpodia
Mighty Studio, San Antonio, Texas
Printed by SmithPrint, San Antonio, Texas

Dedication

These pages are dedicated to the parade of women, and some men, who have had the small stories of your own lives altered by the larger story of the Gospel. It is for you who have been touched, unsettled, and teased by the mysterious intercourse of preaching.

It is for you who have grasped glimpses of your own naked truth in the mirror of preaching and have been, as it were, put on hold. You who have wanted to look again, but thought it impolite to stare; or did not have the courage to look into these subterranean truths alone. This book is for those grappling with the unfinished business of "this certain kind" of impaling preaching, that laid you open, then kissed you good-bye.

Word, which has made a
demand on the most cherished secrets,
collided with the deepest human contradiction, and
ignited a love and a search for the
God who lives God's best life,
in the midst of all our
painful, crooked, gap-toothed, imperfect
stories.

Contents

Acknowledgements

I wish to thank my faithful Executive Director Clara Mitchell for unfailing support, honest feedback and for continuing to hold me to "The Standard." God sent you to me, and I am humbled. Thank you to little Michael and Brian Campbell for letting your mommy come to work some days; Denise, you are still the best Executive Assistant ever! I will appreciate until forever the web of women in my daily space who keep pacing me to accomplish destiny: Shirley Johnson, Elizabeth Manuel, Emma Deloach, Adaku Okoru, Nicki Phillips, Cheryl Henry, Sherry Anderson, Beverly Pillot, Renee Torain, Quida Patterson, Carlotta Miranda and my "Destiny Team" each one.

Diane Hannah, Publisher/Editor-in-Chief of FAITH MAGAZINE, you were my midwife and encourager in the wee hours. The best is yet to come!!

Deep gratitude to Jan Schubert for your editorial wisdom, and the encouragement born of "fresh eyes."

The Greek word "oikos" means "house." From this word comes the English rendering of our words "ecumenical, ecology, and economic." Each of my Destiny Partners worldwide continue to help me build the collective "house" which shelters women who are in process, until their change comes.

Thank you Destiny Partners for embracing all women in the spirit of oneness — ecumenicity; for knowing the value of all our gifts, which keeps this ministry in the natural balance that sustains life — ecology; and for the stewardship of economic promises given, and promises kept.

Thank you my friend, Dr. Renita Jean Weems, the first woman in my life who wrote a real book, and showed me that every woman has at least one real story that some other woman needs to hear.

Finally, thank you David, my husband with whom I have walked through a thousand stories of storms and peaceful seasons, and with whom I still seek joyful endings.

Preface

Life is made up of stories.

Short stories. Almost missed stories.

Stories that have been edited out of consciousness. Forgotten. Stored away like so many snapshots, in a trunk in the attic. Some make us smile wistful, silent smiles. Some stories make us slap our thighs and roar with laughter till our sides hurt; they are stories that beg to be told over and over again. Some terrify and shame us, and seal our lips. Some stories are incomprehensible, and seem not to fit into what we have planned for our larger lives.

And most of the stories that really matter are the ones from inner space — the ones from deep within our souls.

The stories in this book may not hang together, or fit in the order you might expect. They may not be the stories you would expect to hear from a "Pentecostal-preacher-type" or one who poses as a "sanctified scholar" of sorts. No matter. Stories do not always tell themselves in correct order, nor choose their casts predictably. Not in real life. "Knights in shining armor, love and marriage, a baby carriage and happily ever after" may not be your story. Or mine.

Nevertheless, within each life are valuable, sterling short stories. They are not always immediately dramatic or at first, soul stopping. They often are the interjections, the snapshots in which God inserts God's self amid the clutter and then waits. It takes getting older to find the yarn to thread and piece together each short story, and to see what God has been writing. Composing a life.

The outrageous waste of this life is in thinking the only stories that matter are the stories about dead people. Or the stories we read about in the Bible. Or in a novel. Or in a history book. And little do we celebrate the precious worth of the one short story we are living this day.

Never judge your short story by its brightness or its bitterness until the whole tale has been told. The real story. The one written and read from within.

One storyteller put it this way: "It does not yet appear what we shall be; but we know that when He shall appear — when the whole story unfolds — we shall be like Him."

Stories From
INNER
space
Confessions
Of A Preacher Woman and Other Tales

We read

To know that

We

Are not

Alone.

*

C. S Lewis

Introduction

Writing is **medicine.** When I was a girl, I dreamed of becoming a physician. Maybe, because of my frequent ills and maladies, the smells and rhythms of the hospital became familiar, comforting, even intoxicating to me. I wanted to become a surgeon. My admiration became a kind of secret kinship to these men who cut me and excavated my young body and healed me until the next episode. I gave them my love along with my organs. By my graduation from college, I knew that the relentless urgings in my soul would indeed call me to cut, to excavate, to amputate, to engraft and hopefully to heal. But mine was to handle a region of human life far more tricky than the anatomy. As a preacher, mine was to become a physician, a midwife, a caregiver for the soul. *The soul.* This region of human life is not palpable by the hand, nor discernable by scans or x-ray machines. As a preacher of a specific genre, my assignment has not been to summon brimstone, or to slay the sin giants in public displays of deliverance, or to wear sackcloth and ashes, remonstrating over the eternal destiny of the masses. My assignment has not been to take up the sword.

Mine has been to *wield the scalpel.* I have been given the pulpit as my operating theatre and the altar as the healing table for those who would offer and entrust their sickened exposed parts to me, and to God, in hope. The sword is for the masses. The scalpel is for the individual. The sword is for the conqueror. The scalpel is for the one whom life and *dis*-ease has vanquished. It is to dissect and repair the tucked away, soiled, infected stories of the heart and the soul, in light of the larger Eternal Story.

The Gospel message is for the microcosmic private spots. These places, when redeemable, can interpret and give meaning to the whole tale of a woman's life, if anyone cares to notice.

The human soul is a region that must be located and tended by "gifting and calling." The preacher is *called* to reverence this soul. She or he must have the *grace gifts* to love, yes tenderly love the soul, even in its most pathetic condition. We tend the soul, knowing that the soul alone will organize all else of human well-being or human despair, both in this life and beyond.

After 30 years of the *spoken* word, I admit, there has always existed a dangling, nagging bout of unfinished business with every soul I have ever encountered, after every altar call, after each workshop, after each benediction. I am like a mother who releases her newborn child, moist, squirming and fresh from God, into the hands of waiting adoptive parents. These parents, she hopes, will raise her child and love her well. But there is a haunting echo at each birthday, or in the face of each age-appropriate child she meets: "How is *my* child today? Did he survive? Did they treat him kindly? Is she cold ... or hungry? What would she look like by now?"

Evangelistic preaching is an awful act. In spite of our calling and our genuine grace gifts, it is *impaling*. It pulverizes the heart without ever breaking the skin. It is awful in its paradox, precisely because it is at once so intimate, so interior;

and on the other hand, so disengaged, so incomplete. It births, then it abandons. I hasten to acknowledge that all we do, we must do by faith. The Almighty alone is privy to the evolution and final perfecting of the "new creation." Whether absent or present, the preacher can only coach, encourage, rebuke, and exhort the believer. And whether absent or present, we must believe, *by faith*, that our preaching avails, and that the person falls or stands, ultimately, unto God.

That being said, there still remains the unfinished business.

Evangelical, itinerate preaching is an act of hit-and-run, of same day surgery. It is as brutal as it is tender. It is as profoundly disassembling as it is reordering. For these very reasons and others, this kind of preaching begs, yes, *demands*, aftercare.

And so the preacher writes.

Some writing can be medicinal, applied at regular intervals as needed. Some written words can staunch the bleeding and comfort a throb in the heart. Some writing can fondle the scar tissue of old, old stories, calling to mind the awesome wonder of how *any of us* got over, indeed.

Writing is **integration.** To write is to disrobe. It is to invite the voyeurs. To write is to welcome strangers into the private regions of one's life, and to expose the base commonality of us both. The reader gets to pretend that she has not always been curious about "these matters." The writer is afforded the buffer, the anonymity, the drawn shade of the page as she discloses them.

To preach is to offer "The Word" to a crowd who comes, at

least with some predisposition to honor it, to believe it, to handle it with reverence, or to simply reject it outright. While listening to preaching, we as hearers momentarily submerge our criticisms and politely set aside the stuff in "The Word" which baffles us or enrages us. After all, it is "God's," if only by virtue of the fact that it is proclaimed in God's house, under God's roof. Preaching is The Word of The One with far more historical credibility than the human story of the lone preacher. So we nod and we say "Amen."

But to *write* is another story. And I write for *this reading, thinking Christian audience*, not solely about "The Word. " This is about another word. More carnal than divine. More unsettling than comforting. Yet, to write these pages is to make an offering that is in some sense just as "eternal" and certainly just as holy. *The stories of pain and survival and celebration are always sacred. Holy.* Most holy, because *God has been there,* lurking unseen, feverishly at work in the darkness of our unknowing. These pages speak of the human condition — that which *was*, which *is*, and barring divine intervention and sometimes with it — *ever shall be.* To write is to bring some things together, under the same roof. To integrate.

My offering of this book extends the written word, the woman *story*, as a tentative, uncertain hand. I hope that a responsive chord of chemistry will be struck in the heart, in the mind, in the imagination of the reader. It is a terrorizing dance. It is a bashful flirtation. In ways that differ from preaching, the writer alone must bear responsibility for these actions now taken. In ways different than in preaching, the evidence becomes permanent and the blame cannot be shifted to say, "The Bible said it." No, *the preacher said it.*

Now.

Selah.

The aura of the holy desk is bridged. The *life* of the preach-er-writer is offered irretrievably as a slain sacrifice: *bloody, helpless, willing.* Sacrifices must be offered in love alone.

Every preacher must preach.

Some preachers must write to bear witness to what we preach and to walk with others as we collectively and honest-ly sort it out. The nagging, unfinished business of preaching wants to *integrate* the *precursors* of why we preach in the first place, and the *aftermath* of what we have preached. How does it all add up? How does it all fit together, this before-and-after reality?

Writing is a feeble attempt to integrate the "stuff over there" with the "stuff in here." To line up what I know, with what no one else will admit they know, too. It is the courage to bring the stuff from "back yonder" into line with the reali-ty of here and now, and to celebrate that *it took them both* to make us genuine. 'Integrate" comes from the word "integer" or whole number. The woman in me, or in you, cannot be made whole until the past, the present and the future are all given validity. Recognized. Celebrated. Heard. Learned from. Sometimes we cannot risk reassembling our own brokenness until we have witnessed some other woman handling her own "dry bones" and her scattered, disconnected parts. In the pri-vate conversation of the written page — differently than in worship or in preaching — a woman can learn integration watching another woman, piecing parts together under the loving guidance of her God and not being ashamed. The preacher writes for the wholeness we are all seeking.

Writing is **reunion.** Writing is most perplexing when the beloved is faceless. "Which is the audience you shall write for?" they ask. One knows. Not by name or by census. Not by survey or research. I have met this audience over the past 30 years in storefront churches, seminary classrooms, college dormitories, military chapels, cathedrals, correctional institutions, and convention halls. I have come to know them, and to love them one and all, through the dreadful, awful act of preaching. They have kissed my face, and tried to articulate their stories to me, in brief snatches after each benediction. They have trailed me to exits, followed me to parking lots, sought counsel in my hotel rooms and pressed hundreds of crumpled addresses and telephone numbers into my departing hands, with the hope that I could help them finish what God had started. All because this preaching thing made them know ... *that I knew* their untold story ... even if we were never to meet again. These pages are our long overdue reunion.

The audience I write for is the myriad of women, and some men, who have become wedded to me in preaching and in pain; and in the power and proof of survival. They refuse to be contained in a denominational boundary. They will not fit neatly into a class or region or level of learning. They are a tricky bunch, these women, and some men, whose faith has collided head-on with their gross contradictions. Though their faith is now a bit misshapen, maybe non-traditional, and perhaps even a bit irreverent, the faith and *the stories that forged it* somehow have been mysteriously enriched by the collision. These collisions of life and faith have made strong women ... just keep on coming.

I write for you who have set out to synergize a newer, bigger vision of yourselves and your tomorrows. We met long ago, and in these pages we will embrace, and touch again, and kiss each other's faces, though our reunion has seemed improbable. I remember you, since the day I met you long ago in a thousand church pews. I hope you have been emboldened in your "outer space." I pray you were made better in your real life, precisely because of what was conceived in your "inner space" by the "awe"-full, outrageous, foolishness of preaching. But just in case preaching or those testimonies of the dead are still insufficient, I pray these pages may offer some "stories from life" to take into your own tomorrows to give you courage and to keep you strong.

Writing is **for real**. It is for the purpose of enabling genuineness. Even when stories are not factual, they are often *oh so real*. Real is what resonates with a soul. Real is what convicts the "false" flimsy parts of the way we live our lives, or refuse to live them. Real is not something we manufacture, because we *desire* it to be so; real is what corresponds to Truth and lines up with God in our most fundamental knowing. It indicts the hollow ways we worship our God, make love to our mates or handle our children. Real is what nags us, and finally makes us hungry for the *spirit of life*, and dares us to go deeper than opinions of men or approval of onlookers. Real inspires us with the hand of God at our backs, nudging and urging us to reach for more than we have become satisfied with in our pitiful, scared, small ways of doing "life on the surface." Life lived "outside of real" always welcomes the substitutes and illusions that seduce women into bondage.

There was once a Velveteen Rabbit, and in the beginning, he was really splendid. He was fat and bunchy, as a rabbit should be; his coat was spotted and brown and white; he had real thread whiskers; and his ears were lined with pink sateen. On Christmas morning when he sat wedged in the tip of the boy's stocking with a sprig of holly between his paws, the effect was charming. ... For at least two hours the boy loved him. ... Then in the excitement of all the other new toys, the Velveteen Rabbit was forgotten.

For a long time he lived in the toy cupboard, and no one thought much about him. He was naturally shy, and being made only of velveteen, some of the more expensive toys quite naturally snubbed him. The mechanical toys were very superior ... the model boats ... even the jointed wooden lion ... and between them all the little rabbit was made to feel himself very insignificant and commonplace. The only person who was kind to him was the Skin Horse.

The Skin Horse had lived longer in the nursery than any of the others. He was so old that his brown coat was bald in patches, and showed the seams underneath, and most of the hairs in his tail had been pulled out to string bead necklaces. He was wise, for he had seen one long succession of mechanical toys arrive, to boast and swagger, and one by one, break their mainsprings and pass away. He knew they were only toys, and would never turn into anything else.

"What is REAL?" asked the rabbit one day when they were lying side by side in the nursery before Nana came to tidy up. "Does it mean having things that buzz inside you and a stick-out handle?"

"Real isn't how you are made," said the Skin Horse. "It's a thing that happens to you. When a child loves you a long, long time, not just to play with, but really loves you, then you become Real."

"Does it hurt?" asked the Rabbit.

"Sometimes," said the Skin Horse, for he was always truthful. "When you are Real, you don't mind being hurt."

"Does it happen all at once, like being wound up?" he asked, "Or bit by bit?"

"It doesn't happen all at once," said the Skin Horse. "You become. It takes a long time. That's why it doesn't happen often to people who break easily, or who have sharp edges, or who have to be carefully kept. Generally by the time you become Real most of your hair has been loved off, and your eyes drop out and you get loose in the joints and very shabby. But these things don't matter at all, because once you are Real, you can't be ugly, except to people who don't understand."[1]

To write *truthfully* is to defy a culture of silence. It is to risk the ugly parts, knowing that some, who are *not* real, will not

---

[1] (Excerpts: The Velveteen Rabbit by Margery Williams. Running Press, Philadelphia 1989. Used by Permission)

understand. No matter. As Christians of the Evangelical/Pentecostal/Charismatic variety, I suspect there are some things we are not supposed to know about ourselves, much less say aloud. But the truth we are *willing to know* is the only truth that will make us free.

We are becoming new creatures in the spiritual core. Yet in doing so, some Christians have learned to compartmentalize our history from our everyday realities. We have learned to discard our own stories. They fall fretfully into the blind spot. *That* was then, and *this* is now, we say. But "woman reality" does not melt into yesterday's history and disappear. It rides alongside her in the blind spot until the inevitable emotional, psychological or sometimes physical collision takes place. Old encoded experiences lurk somewhere beneath the new "learned" church behaviors. Then one day we are ambushed, and we cannot figure out where "this old stuff" came from. It (woman reality) refuses to remain camouflaged beneath our newest expensive suit, or grander diamond rings or our latest model car. It refuses to hide any longer beneath the facade of our "prosperity," just as it will not remain quiet, marginalized by our poverty. ***It is about a desire to be Real***, as the Skin Horse said. Our humanity brazenly defies our "spirituality" because she, the real woman, has been ignored, scorned, or silenced in the newfound religious ecstasy that excludes the genuine parts. Her whole reality begs to be integrated into the whole of life. Not dissected, swept under a rug and denied in shame. Every woman's story deserves to be told, if only to herself. It is the principle thing that makes her "real."

Finally, this writing is about the courage it takes to stimulate *dialogue.*

In all my years of Christian training, I learned propriety, correctness and holiness. Also, I well-mastered the art of self-censorship. Christians generally learn by monologue, the one-way talk from pulpit to pew. In Christian matters, we seldom move to a larger opportunity. Preachers are always talking; women find ourselves always listening, or at least, seeming to. I have been on both sides of the equation; and neither is satisfying to the soul without the other.

It has been the challenge of my adult years to free myself from self-censorship and to allow genuine connections to emerge — beyond the preaching persona. In the church I learned early that truth was punishable by death. I learned that some experiences were so unacceptable, some opinions or perspectives so arousing to the saints, that these had to be cut off, cut out and thrown away. They were not "compatible" with this new life in Christ Jesus — nor with those who were His spokespersons. Because I despised being alone, ignored or excommunicated for the truths I told, I chose to become dishonest. Whether preaching, or in private dialogue, I mastered submission and silence. I grew tired of the fight to remain connected because of the truths I challenged. The need for approval can cause one to barter away one's very soul.

Any actor can pass words. But **dialogue without truth** deflates the passion of the exchange. With age, one discerns the contexts and chooses the battles for truth telling. With wisdom, a woman becomes less likely to allow herself to be branded a "rebel" simply because she demands respect. With age and wisdom, one thing becomes more and more clear. Dialogue is air. Whether in a stale marriage, an awkward friendship, or in fearful religion, dialogue is air. Truth is oxygen. It takes immense courage for some of us to tell the truth we know. You will tire quickly of suffocating in appropriate silence.

Writing and reading are ongoing possibilities to integrate truth, to rekindle passion and give birth to connection between the woman and the people in her religious space. "Dialogue" within the life of the church in general, or the black Pentecostal church in particular, has often struggled like an awkward adolescent — expressing itself at one extreme or another. In handling deep human truth on one hand, *we vomit it* unreflectively, angrily, like a fitful teenager. Preachers or pew members, given the opportunity, may verbally disrobe like strippers on stage to the applause of an aroused audience. We brutalize hearers with our repressed rage, our scalding judgments, our compassionless standards (we call them testimonies or sermons depending on the speaker). And there you have it ladies and gentleman: "truth."

Conversely, we are totally and sullenly silent. Whether white male Catholic priests struggling with sexual disorders, or black, poor Pentecostal women struggling against invisibility, we tend to retreat into our own private spaces, to ruminate, wrestle down and sanitize our own truth. We dare not appear to contradict "holiness" or "righteousness" or the currently accepted notion of "virtue." We nod, smile, move our lips ... and bring forth wind.

And *we hope* someone else will aid us.

We hope someone else will say for us what we were indeed thinking all along.

Church women are silent about what we know to be true, lest it precipitate emotional violence against us, from the powers that be. We learn safe dishonesty in the presence of the men we want to love us: our superiors, our pastors, our husbands, daddies, bosses, lovers, as well as the women we want to approve of us and include us into their circles.

Truthful dialogue takes courage. Alas, we are modern Christians, conversant with gadgets and electronic relationships, but victims of our own overwhelming cowardice. Then one day, we get too old or too tired, or we grow too isolated from the game to be frightened by the judges.

When a woman has faith in God she can choose to extend that faith to other humans. Indeed, may these pages prompt your search, and cause you to believe that there are real people who can hear, really hear, and care about the stories from a real *life. Faith gives us courage to speak up.* To a husband. To child. To a therapist. To a long dead parent. To whomever needs to hear you.

> *Let your women keep silence in the church;*
> *for it is not permitted for them to speak.*
> *(St. Paul to the Corinthians)*

Permitted. Trained. Christian women and some men wake up and realize we have reappeared far too long in pew, in pulpit, or in life, *mute*. We mimed. We *acted out* the messages, the buried stories we dared not speak. The preacher writes to invade the deadness of rich entombed realities.

The preacher invites her reader into a safe corner of the room, offers a cushioned chair and a soft light. The preacher writes in order to create a place for dialogue in silenced, impacted hearts.

Read these chapters at great risk.

They might make you think. Scarier still, they might make you *talk;* confess to yourself what is real. They might prompt you to find another person, and speak out loud about the thoughts, the experiences, the old, precious, hidden stories you are discovering from your own "inner space."

Go in with me. Here too, is God.

The stupid either forgive or forget.
The naïve forgive and forget.
The wise forgive but they do not forget.

Thomas Szasz

In Paris there is a monument to the French who died in German concentration camps. I was horrified by the inscription over the door.

"Let us forgive but never let us forget."

All of a sudden I realized that the real virtue came in forgiving precisely while remembering. For if I could forget, then forgiving would not ever be necessary.

Virginia Elizondo

Forgive us our trespasses as we forgive others.

Jesus, as He taught his disciples to pray

Chapter One
Hush

How do you make a woman? You begin with a little girl. Except for Mother Eve, every woman is, in time or in history, someone's little girl. The woman you are is the outline, the tracing of the little girl you were. The woman you were raised by, the one you married, or live with, the woman you love or leave is herself the beneficiary or the victim. Childhood events and people conspired together to "make her." This momentum of childhood events will not be barricaded, no, not even behind spiritual boundaries. Salvation does not alter the facts of a woman's historical past. It can, thank God, impact the future *consequences* of those facts when the woman lets God handle *her whole* life story.

After salvation, an unsaved child of incest by her grandfather, is a saved child — who was *still violated* by her grandfather. Were you the child who was *abandoned* by her mother, or who went about raggedy, hungry or stinking and ashamed *with* a mother? Did you drown in the apathy of an environment that simply tolerated you because they were all preoccupied with just surviving? Were you given a life context that never celebrated your coming, and hence never missed you when you left? What of the child who was hurt by the people who should have loved her? She ached for touch, for feather kisses and mommy games, but instead was met with fists, belts, dark closets, or worse? Or what becomes of the child who was raised by a mentally ill or drunken or violent parent?

Maybe you were the child who was *loved and adored* by the most doting and generous family. You are only able to guess at the reasons for other women's tears. Eventually, you *will* know. Could you have been the child, well loved and well wanted, who still could not escape wandering in the secret minefields of growing up female and vulnerable?

Whatever.

Now as women we must decide what to do with the *facts* and the *emotional information* that those facts carry.

Salvation changes many things — our position before God, our choices, our attitudes, and prayerfully, our behaviors and our eternal destiny. But salvation does not change the facts of a woman's history. Some of childhood's marks are permanent. It takes a real God to rearrange those marks on the paper, and turn them into something that makes sense.

Some preachers believe their task is to aid a woman in sanitizing her past; forgetting her history; compartmentalizing her reality into the "before Christ" and "since-salvation" dualities. *This preacher's job* is to help a woman *utilize* her history before God, knowing that none of this caught God by surprise.

Some women learn from history, and become wise.

Some women testify (honestly) to history, and become guards and guides for our daughters.

Or some women are shamed by our history and bury it, and reinforce that burial with the rituals of church life and rhetoric of "God talk." We re-label our histories with such invented terms as "generational curses;" we blame; we distance; we become emotionally deformed. But far too often, we do not heal.

The little girl inside every woman continues to make demands. The 12-year-old mortally wounded daughter of Jairus becomes, in some sense, the adult woman whose life is still bleeding, seeping, oozing out of her (Luke 8:40ff). "She," the wounded girl, must be attended to, or the woman will never have rest. Under stress, the woman will revert to old patterns of childhood coping: she will take to her bed, or withdraw, or pout and throw temper tantrums. She may run away from home; leave first always, to avoid 'being left' by anyone ever again. She may become the selfless, good girl, hoping to win favor from mama and daddy and other authority figures. When she feels alone and comfortless, she may crawl into the arms or the lap of whoever is waiting or welcoming. When afraid, she may strike out, curse, or physically fight, because that is what frightened little girls do. To be sure, this little girl always shows up at the most unexpected time. And she is sure to embarrass the woman.

In Grown Folks' Business

For decades I have encountered such women in church.

Grown women. Fully formed women. Strong women. Woman who wrestle down the little girl in themselves, and refuse to know her. I have watched them; studied them; walked behind them, eavesdropping. My first memory of church is as a child, embedded in woman-ness. It is a memory of my caretaker, old Mrs. Daughtery, the wife of the assistant minister. My head lay on the lap of this old woman, who was fanning me, patting me, *hushing me* through peppermint smells and strains of stilted organ music in the Methodist church. In some sense, women are the matrix upon which we have church. We build our usher boards and choirs and committees and Sunday schools upon the love and commitment of women. Whether in storefronts or cathedrals, at bus stops, walking or driving BMW's; single, married, lesbian, professional or working class; saints, seekers or sinners — women's differences are eclipsed by one larger reality: *The unfinished work of the childhoods that produced us* and our collective reluctance to tell ourselves the truth about it all.

The work we must finish in the church is to admit them — these childhood issues — and to dare to create a safe context to air them out. Women must provide a safe space for the "little girl's" voice to be heard. As children, we are sometimes too ashamed to admit, or to speak up about what has happened to us. So we store experiences away in the vaults of our child-minds. Experiences need explanation.

Interpretation.

Processing.

Conclusions.

But as children, we possess neither the tools, nor the tutors. We are moved on to the next thing, the next grade, the new neighborhood school — and unfinished emotional business is further sealed away. For seasons, it is almost as if we have forgotten. And if we dared to broach certain subjects, there was, in the vernacular of the 1950's-colored-people's family system, the notion of young girls being "in grown folks' business."

"Hush."

There ended the inquiry.

Things that have been hushed go underground. For some of us, the issues re-emerge at the front door of the church. Indeed, some of us find genuine regeneration. Yet so many women who seek the church's embrace do so because we have been broken, and are in need of repair. We come *thinking* it is God we seek, when we are merely seeking relief. We come because we are damaged and in danger of collapse. Only later do we make the connection between our personal pain and the larger eternal issues of original sin, redemption, and salvation. We come broken, and mostly want first aid.

What no one tells us is that some "breaks" take a lifetime to heal.

"I'll walk you home," he said. "It's getting dark and you don't want to be walkin' by yourself." She straightened her back and tried to act confidently, like she had done this before. Public School #53 had just dismissed the neighborhood pilot program for evening classes for these so-called underprivileged kids. Eight-thirty was not considered late at all for kids in this part of town, even if they were only 6th, 7th and 8th graders. She was never really all that sure of herself. A few people seemed to like her okay, but she was certainly not in the center of things. Not like the girls who had their hair permed or wore coordinated clothes. Big for her age, glasses and all, she was pretty average. That perhaps is why it was all the more startling when "he" asked to walk her home. "Well, okay ..." she hesitated. The little girl was ashamed to admit that her father did not allow her to "take company," but she did not know how to refuse without looking more awkward than she was beginning to feel. He was one of the big boys that

hung around their school. She knew his name and his face. All the girls did, because he was "fine" and went to high school and dressed real nice.   She had seen him at the corner store that they all visited daily to exchange a cigarette butt or buy a 10-cent dill pickle or some Mary Janes or Mike and Ike candies to smuggle into school, or to meet and pair up for the walk home. She had seen him at the corner store, and stolen glances at his face. Now this evening, he fell into stride with her steps, the big boy did. And he began to talk to her. No boy ever did that before. His words seemed to tumble from his mouth effortlessly.   But she could only look straight ahead. Or down at her feet, which felt so big, so clumsy, disconnected from her brain and trotting along with a momentum of their own. She nervously shoved the cat-eyed glasses up on her nose, and tried to ignore the funny airless feeling at the fringe of her head. "Oh yeah, this here is my boy Earl. You don't mind if he walk with us..." As Earl fell into step on the other side of her, she was in some kind of suspended state. She was hydroplaning on the words of the two big boys walking her home, straining, gawky, trying to fill out a big-girl moment. She was scared, anticipating the trouble she would be in when she reached her house. With not one, but two boys. She was envisioning the picture window where her daddy sat, and took in a panoramic view of all that happened on that side street approaching their corner house. But when they said, "Let's take the long way home, just around the block..." her jumbled girlish thoughts collided in her head. "He likes me. Wonder if the other girls see them walking me? I am gonna be in troouuuuoubbblle. They are really big boys..." And on the dialogue went in her head. Her heart was pounding, but she was too inexperienced to discern the difference between excite-

ment and dread. They felt like the same thing. Her feet were keeping pace. Past the turn-off to home.

The two boys began to talk to each other; something was vaguely funny to them. But the girl could not quite get it. "Oh, let me just run into my house right here, and tell my Moms I am walking you. You can come on up. My Moms is cool. Come on and meet her."

And her disconnected feet walked her up the flights of stairs. They passed the locked/unlocked/locked doors into the silent, unmothered flat. The two of them, big boys and the little girl. The boy turned on the television, unnaturally loud she thought. They offered her Kool-Aid. And their talk turned a sickly sweet, like the Kool-Aid. She wanted to go, please. In the light she saw every detail in grotesque relief ... things she had never noticed at the school corner store.

Or maybe she saw the things which terror magnifies.

The big red bumps on his yellow face. The narrow rugged hawk of his nose. The faint smell of gas from the not-at-home-mother's stove. His big hot hands as they came, multiplied, it seemed, from all directions. She tried to laugh and pretend he was not really serious, and could she please gohomenowpleeeaaase. Like a movie on fast-forward, a blur, a flash. Though it whizzes past, it is constructed by definable frames. When her head hit the kitchen cabinet. When his big hand groped over her small breast. When her glasses flew off and landed under the red vinyl kitchen chair. When his mouth hurt her lips. When shame arose in her throat like hot vomit as her body parts were exposed. When she felt that first awful steel against her. It was an object, unfamiliar, but immediately recognizable as a weapon about to be unleashed against her with no pity. From that floor in that kitchen, she looked sideways at the boy Earl who stood as a silent sentry at the door. She searched his face for a glimmer of something that would arouse him as an ally, a rescuer from this awful moment. She hoped for a mother to appear from some corner, some back room — a mother who would adjourn this clandestine torture and let her run free. "He said his mother was at home???" Her daddy would make this big boy leave her alone, but ... this jumbled, shameful confusion could never straighten itself upright in her head. How could the little girl flee to her daddy's comfort ... when somehow she believed she would be blamed for this ... thing. The fear and smells and pain stood juxtaposed to the dread of her daddy's anger. Daddy's anger. Daddy's anger. Daddy's...

Then her racing thoughts were bludgeoned into silence. At that moment she knew that there would be no rescue. Thomas Moore has said that the word "hymen" and "hymn" have the same derivation in Latin. Both signify a "gate" which leads to pleasure and to life. The big boy was on her like a thousand trampling bulls, battering her virginal gates. Gated pleasure places. Designed by the little girls' God for the patient and delighting hand of covenant love and honor. Trampled. Plundered. Ruined. The first crush of pain radiated like lightening bolts up her spine. Lightening struck and exploded in her loins and radiated across her hips, and engulfed her legs and feet till she wondered if she would ever walk again. When he stood over her and kicked her, she did not even feel his foot crash into her. "Shut up that damn noise." So by the time the second boy Earl stood over her on that floor, she was "shut up," and she was shut down.

Hushed.

She now seemed to watch it all from some other place. Perched like an elf, she was atop the not-at-home-mother's-refrigerator, with a detached curiosity. "That little girl is crying." "What is that thing going into her body?" "Look at all that red stuff ... she must be ... hurt ... she's bleeding. Why is he hurting her? She is really going to be in trouble now."

Three blocks seemed 3,000 miles in the darkness. And the pain. Lord, have mercy! Every step was pain. It was the only reminder that she was still inside herself. Her chest was full of tears and something she could not put words to. Her body was inhaled, suspended somewhere; so full she had to remember to breathe. She hurt, and mindlessly her pain propelled her through the darkness of the city street, trying to get home. The little girl so much needed home; she was so thankful for the refuge she had always trusted, a place called home. And now for the first time in her young life, she was afraid to arrive at home. She wondered if the telltale heart that was breaking between her legs, the strange new feeling of blood and shame, would shout aloud about her spoiling. She fumbled with her key and tried to look normal as she, guilty of being hurt, skulked into the parent's house. Alone, dazed, disheveled. But no one seemed to notice much of anything, between the Ed Sullivan Show and the latest crisis with a roomer who had not paid his rent. Why was she late? School tomorrow. Was she hungry? Go to bed. She slipped between their words and made her way upstairs to the bathroom, where she sat on the toilet for a long, long time, and tended her wounds as best she knew how. She choked down her tears and her terror and began the process of burying her shame.

Wash.

WASH.

School tomorrow.

Hush.

Don't cry.

Smother the hurt with your rage.

Fight.

It does not matter whom.

Strike back, and hope you hit it.

Be angry and sin, but only against yourself.

But Hush. Don't cry.

Sicken.

Decay inwardly. Tubercular. Rheumatic.

Depress.

Try to die.

If that does not work,

Perform.

Be the best.

Hush.

"Wash in The Blood."

Be holy.

Cry, but only in church and believe it's the "spirit."

Achieve.

Hush.

Don't ask anyone for anything.

Weep, but only in private.

Don't draw too much attention to yourself.

Hush.

Make everyone else proud.

Let everyone else cry on you.

Hush, now.

Protect yourself.

Don't hurt your Mama.

You're all right.

Don't tell your Daddy, no telling what he will do.

Shhhhh.

Don't go beneath the surface.

But if you do, for God's sake don't mention what you find.

Hush, child.

Forget what is behind.

Keep growing.

Sing!

Sing LOUD!!

Find a hushed man.

Get married.

Both of you look straight ahead.

Keep going.

Preach.

Preach GOOD.

Dress Good.

Look Good.

Live GOOD.

Never stop too long or look too hard.

Never ask God why.

Hush.

Let the tears pool just beneath the surface of your heart, and carry them a lifetime.

Protect yourself.

Take care of yourself.

But whatever you do ... just Hush.

The little girl neatly sealed away her horrors and never uncorked them again for the next 33 years.

Rape is a soul-altering secret to carry at any age.

It is especially devastating when you have just turned 11 years old.

I look into the window and I see the

Light.

I move in and out of your mind as you

Read.

I hover over your bed

All night.

And I hear you

Cry

And I wish you knew.

That I am in Heaven

Where little babies never

Die.

Message in a dream from my un-conceived,
never born child, 1978.

Chapter Two
I Have No Child

I need a future to hand my life to.

I have no child. No butterfly kick shall ever disturb my slumbering womb. I shall never know the weight of breasts, bulbous and lactating, searching for the ravenous little mouth to complete the private gestalt. I have no child.

No daughter who will learn from my lessons. No daughter to watch me for cues. I have no little girl to dress in frilly lace and experiment with her hair and to witness as her body expresses itself into shy womanhood. I will never spy my own form in later models or updated versions, in my daughter's face or hands or bosom. I will never have the chance to feign irritation as my daughter percolates through my life with treasures she excavated from my closets and dresser drawers, saying, "Mama, I didn't think you would mind ..." I will never be party to the initiations of adulthood; never comfort her when her heart is broken; never watch with puzzled exclusion the bond between her and her daddy. I shall never have a daughter to tutor in the daily-ness of constructing a home and setting a table and calibrating one's intuition about how much seasoning to use in the sauce. I have no daughter to protest her forays into too-soon love, or hear mama-can't-you-understand? defenses. I am ripe with wisdom and bursting with love. I am blessed with adored God-daughters and beautiful nieces and devoted spiritual offspring. But I have no daughter.

And I have no son. My brothers were never born. My father died too soon. I have never known boys. Not really known them. What would it have meant to carry a man-child in the womb? What thoughts would I have had of him, to make him strong or gentle ... rambunctious or reflective? Needless. I have no son. How I would have longed for a son to give my adoration to, and stand apart from in his different-ness. A boy child, to hand to his father, for far-too-soon initiations and excursions into barbershops and ball games, and then to demand his return, smilingly. I have no son to be proud of at his first athletic victory or to be jealous over when he discovers the first girl that he loves more than his mother; to watch him grow thick and sinewy; to smell his man smells, and still to know when, like a little boy, he needed the refuge and retreat of his Mama's space. I would have hoped the lessons he learned from me would soften and tend the life of the women in *his* future. That he would genuinely like them. I have no son, whose release into larger life would have been my terrorized initiation into an unknown realm of prayer. Unrelenting, pre-conscious prayer. Mother-for-son interces-sion, standing as the only sentry against his incarceration, his addiction or his murder.

Mary, I see you better now, there at the
foot of the cross.
Hovering at the mouth of your own bereavement.
"Woman, behold thy son!"

I remain childless. I have no son, who when I grow old, I can look to for security, lean on for comfort, pester to visit me more often, or call me more faithfully. I would hope to have loved him well, bequeathing him memories of good smells and satisfied appetites. There would have been candied yams and mustard greens, macaroni and cheese and corn bread, and fried chicken at raucous Sunday dinner gatherings. I think I would have left him wholesome tastes and mother-wit to strengthen his life after mine is over. These experiences, I fantasize, would hold me in honor with my grandchildren when I am only a memory. "Nana." "Granny." "Big Momma." "Grammy."

But, I have no son.

Though I am older now, my breasts are still heavy and burdened, lactating with dreams that would nourish, stories that would make you laugh out loud, and sacrifices that would be joyfully offered. But, alas, I have no child.

In my twenties, it was a bothersome notion that would ultimately resolve itself. After all, "Delays are not denials," they told me. And, "You have your ministry to prepare for," they consoled me. The awkwardness I felt at the news of a girl-friend's pregnancy, or my chronic absences at the baby showers of the sisters I loved were camouflaged by my work. But in my thirties, with every passing year, the weight of the emptiness pressed in upon me like slow smothering death, inescapable in every lunar cycle. Until at last I knew. Despite the prophets, the prayer warriors and the seers, I knew. There would be no child.

Could any words articulate such a relentless longing? On the obvious level, there is a profound sense of failure. I am a woman, unable to replicate the most fundamental tasks of female biology. I fail to do on purpose what most women accomplish by accident. I found ways to survive, then to dodge the stinging rebuke of older women who judged me as selfish and unspiritual because I "withheld my womb from birthing" in favor of my education, my ministry or as they called it, my "ambition." They never stopped to consider me: My profound failure. How does one discuss loving a man, like Elkanah was with Hannah, who tried in his own way to be "better to her than ten sons" (I Samuel 1:8). Yet to live under the prevailing cloud of uncertainty, the hunch, that perhaps he would have been happier with Peninah, who could have borne him children. Only another involuntarily childless woman could know the sense of outrageous irony every time I read of a newborn baby found in the trash dumpster, or the 14-year-old girl who is brought to my office because she is pregnant for the second time. It is a miracle of grace to restrain the torrent of my own heart, listening to the "Pastor, as-Christians-should-we-get-her-another-abortion??" questions.

"I have no child." I live in a world whose politics let children perish from hunger and disease by the millions, annually. I am formed from the first generation of women who took pills *not* to conceive children. We were the generation of women who normalized as our "rights," the choice to scoop unripe babies from our wombs and discard them as debris. Fetal matter. This is a society that ignores children, mis-educates them, sexually violates them, lets them go hungry and homeless in the midst of affluence. "No Child." This is an empty mantra. Who would care? Why bother?

Childlessness is a prohibited sorrow.

But even when one detours the grief and refuses to *feel* it any longer, it exists as a protest of heart and mind. It runs deeper than the obvious feminine disappointments. It is life wanting itself. When denied, it leaves a vacancy that rebounds with an echo. A slight but persistent keep-coming-up-again-keep-coming-up-again-keep-coming-up-again-ever-so-often pain in the womb of one's life. Silent wailing. Prevailing. Longing. Life wanting itself, as Kahlil Gibran writes. *You should be over that, after all these years. You are the envy of so many women. You have so much. You've accomplished so much. You're loved by so many.* In spite of what they think, life is still wanting itself; not a job or fame or another adorn-ment. Life wanting itself.

"You should be over that by now." In some respects you are. For this mothering place is an old ache that becomes compan-ionable. An injury you learn to live with daily and speak of seldom. It will not totally expire. Like a fire, one has to wait for the years to let it burn low. By the forties, it is a wistful, philosophical grief that makes one cry unshed tears in secret; or be ambushed by scenes of a toddler's eye piercing the childless woman over his mama's shoulder. One learns to give birth to non-living offspring in print or in preaching. Psychologists call it sublimation. The saints call it predestina-tion, God's will. By the forties, one no longer feels compelled to call it anything. You do not offer an explanation of the childlessness, and by now, none is expected. And by the for-ties, one has become noddingly tolerant of the platitudes. "Chile, you can have one of mine..." "You are so lucky not to have children, that way you can do what you want to with your life, your ministry, your ... fill-in-your blank." "There are so many children here who need your love," they admonish. "You can still adopt," they tell me. "Children break your heart honey," they intone. *And to a woman, they all have children of their own.*

But it is not as though one pushes a cart through a grocery store aisle, or browses the department store racks to connect with a person, to bequeath one's life and love and dreams to.

No one has heard me, no, not one.

Whispers

The heart of a mother whispers to her, even if her loins have never produced offspring. *Does one get too old for children to matter?* Listen for the heart of Hannah, and the child that would not come.

> *"So it was year by year — Hannah wept and did not eat.*
> *And she was in bitterness of soul and wept in anguish.*
> *Then she made a vow and said, "O Lord of hosts, if you*
> *will indeed look on the affliction of your maidservant*
> *and remember me, and not forget your maidservant but*
> *will give your maidservant a male child, then I will give*
> *him to the Lord all the days of his life — And Hannah*
> *poured out her soul. Her lips moved but there was no*
> *sound"*
>
> *(I Samuel 1).*

There was no sound.

Who could hear? *I have no child.*

What of Bathsheba? She has no voice, and survives only as a whisper, a side bar in the story of a powerful man. We must discern her plight through her narrator.

"And the Lord struck the child that Uriah's wife bore to
David, and it became ill ... David pleaded with God for
the child ...[But] On the seventh day it came to pass that
the child died"
(II Samuel 12).

What does a mother feel when her child is caught, wedged between God's anger and his parents' sin? Call it adultery or addiction, call it lust or self-absorption, nonetheless she conceives in the midst of dysfunction. Her own. Her man's. Her situations'. Now, how does a mother live with herself suspecting that the sins of the parents are landing on the head of her child; sins that she cannot ever undo, in spite of all her repentance? How does she love and openly grieve the child, born with AIDS, born addicted to crack cocaine, born with her brain circuits scrambled, knowing she is in some way directly responsible? How does a mother connect with the child she will never be able to keep?

Father, forgive me, for I knew what I was doing.

Now, I have no child.

How does she openly grieve the child's death, whom she was not supposed to conceive in the first place, from the man she should never have been with from the start? What is the formula for peace when guilt is competing against Grace? Who can hear a mother whisper for compassion when her mouth is not moving?

The prophet Elisha listens to the widow's whisper:

"Your servant, my husband, is dead.
And now the creditors are coming
to take away my sons..."
(II Kings 4).

To what lengths will a mother go to cancel an unjust burden on her children's lives? Daddies die too soon, or leave too early. Daddies stay sometimes, with an unexpected, sorrowful inability to "pay" what children, or the baby's Mama needs. The children can only wonder. The things they need to know they will learn only when they are old women with children themselves.

Mama, why did you stay with him all those years?

Or sometimes they will learn far sooner than they should have. Pregnant girls. Teen mothers. Statistics. Predictable ghetto girls or middle class disappointments.

Baby, Grandma understands,
That you really loved that man.
Put yourself in Jesus' hands.

So mothers stay. And daddies leave or die, or just never reappear. And children, or someone, must pay. Some children pay a grown-up debt they do not owe, with a price they cannot afford. They become the emotional surrogates to needy mothers, filling their daddy's shoes, when they never even met the daddy.

I have no child, she whispers. Maybe for some women, that *is a good thing.*

"Help me, Elisha!" Mamas are left to figure out what to sell, or give away, or barter or manipulate, or negotiate or create, to keep the creditors of life from imprisoning her children. Will she barter food stamps or steal from the welfare? Will she lend her body to her "men friends" for a little help? Will she swallow pride, and absorb pity; will she put her own dreams on deep freeze; dreams that her children never imagine she could have dreamed for herself? Will she defer college indefinitely, work two or three jobs and make fatigue the one lover she knows best? Or will she make deals with the preacher named Elisha? There are some things a mother can only whisper. There are some lengths to which only a mother will go. Judge her or not. She does not hear you. It is for her child.

And there are the whispers of my own memory.

In inner city Atlanta, at the Grady Memorial Hospital, I am being baptized into the amazing world of poor, marginalized and struggling mothers who have only love to offer. I am a young chaplain in training, assigned to the neo-natal high-risk nursery.

I have no child.

I cannot become pregnant, and here I am in the mix. Giving myself to what is withheld from me. Babies, sick and grasping for life, are everywhere. And their constant mothers are fixtures on the ward with breast pumps and milk offerings, crucifixes and holy water, anointing oil and prayer cloths, and babies who died nonetheless in 1978.

I am called to the side of the Witherspoon family. They want to see their dead baby. In the fifth month of pregnancy, the child slid out of her mother's incompetent uterus into this world, unable to draw her first breath. The second day after the birth, they demand to see this baby and they will not be deterred. What they do not know is that the baby is now entombed in a formaldehyde jar in the basement morgue. As the chaplain, it is my job to find a way to minister to their need, and their need is to find closure to this gaping womb-wound.

I dutifully enter the morgue, masked, gowned and gloved, and retrieve the child, fishing her out of a large glass jar. Her little limbs must be unfolded, coaxed away from her little body with sucking sounds. I place her gently onto a receiving blanket, and wrap her as prettily as possible. She is cold. Rubbery. Perfect little hands. Even little eyelashes. I think about the colored doll-babies I played with as a child. Or the fuzzy little baby heads I have nuzzled, smelling like Johnson's baby lotion in the pink bottle. But this little baby is reeking of the chemical that will preserve her tiny body for the scientific curiosity of this "teaching hospital." I carry her gray and shriveled little body to her parents in the maternity ward. She is too light in my arms to register as a real baby. But indeed, a baby she is. I surrender her to her parents. As if at an altar, the two of them huddle over her with their backs to me, and to the world.

This is a moment so private that only God is invited to watch.
I spy the mommy and daddy as they bend over her, examining her, speaking in low tones to one another. Together they tenderly clothe her in a pink dress they had purchased, no doubt, for her homecoming. There will be a homecoming, but she will be absent as the guest of honor. She gets to wear, one time, this pink outfit that she will never, never grow into. They hold her close. They examine her, and dream for the moment of who she might have

become. They kiss her and grudgingly say good-bye.

And they pay no attention at all to the piercing smell of the formaldehyde. To them, she is all baby smells and infant powder. Their eyes do not register the grotesqueness of the little creature, with wrinkles and gray sloughing skin. To them, she is only beauty.

I still hear the whispers in my mind: *When your child matters to you, desperately loved and wanted, the child is all that matters.*

For the involuntarily childless woman, do children ever cease to matter? For you who *are mothers*, with children on your breast, or your knee, in the next room or away at college; grown and gone across the country or across town with their own lives ... do children, *your children*, still register on the radar of your heart?

To be certain, they matter.

But do they *know today* how much they matter to you?

After all these years, can you still be arrested by the perfectly formed fingers of a stranger's baby who sits next to you on a bus or on a plane? Can you still be moved by the knowing resolute yawn of the infant who will choose sleep over the company of any adoring intruder? Do you ever stop to spy the large piercing toddler eyes that fasten unashamedly on your face in the waiting room? Do you have a moment for the preschooler who has not yet been contaminated by his parents' fear of race, or a so-called stranger — who comes to show you her toy and ask your name? They may be little old souls in miniature bodies. They are not yet spoiled by the socialization or the isolation of their parents. Mother, have you been bored and sated by the wonder of it all, or can you still be humbled by their innocence and their love? Can you still be *instructed* by little children? They are not yet robbed of the joy of touch, or the comfort of welcoming flesh, or the belief that if they cry, the world will respond to their need. Mother, who do you touch? Who do you welcome? Who do you unashamedly need? Who makes your eyes light up when they enter your room?

Will I ever be too old for children to matter? I still sneak fantasy glances at the beautiful young prom queens and the well-mannered departing college jocks and think, "That could be my daughter." "If I could choose a son, my son would be like him."

Look around us at the children. These are our beneficiaries, these babies who remain. Wanted children. Children who were welcomed, even if at first reluctantly. They are souls who have entered history from the realms of God. They are God's idea that life is still worth a try. They will be a conduit to a future that we can only imagine.

These babies, these children, these young people will be handed the cracked, broken, mellowed, renewing dreams of their mamas and daddies; and the dreams of us *who might have been* their parents. This, in essence, is all we have to offer them. These dreams, our love, and a faith that infuses them with spirit-wind, will carry them over their certain impossibilities.

And this will be the stuff, the fodder, the raw material they will use to construct a *life*. However imperfect, this stuff will make them strong. And eventually wise. It will give them kindling for their own fires. These children will inherit our hand-me-down dreams, half-told stories, resurrected hopes, and prayers. They will be rich and textured, edited and torn in places, but the stuff with which to start.

Every woman deserves a beneficiary. It is absurd to contemplate one's own ending, without knowing for sure that

the toil and trouble

the secrets and

the synthesis and

stumbling and the stories and

hard-won lessons will have no safe repository.

I do not want to die, not knowing for sure that my life will matter for some other person's beginnings.

Children matter. How incredibly they matter!

And, you see, I have no child.

Do not just read the Times.

Read the eternities.

*

She who rides a tiger is not afraid to dismount.

African Proverb

Chapter Three
When Your Breast Is Out To Kill You

Graying. Mellowed. Richer.
Knowing finally what life is.
When flesh is not what your life's all about,
You'd be surprised at what you can
Live without.

Our mothers and fathers are dying, or becoming infirm. "Mama fell and broke her hip." "Daddy keeps wandering off, getting lost; we had to hide the car keys from him." "Mother is just not the same since her stroke." We are making hard decisions about nursing homes or moving parents into our own homes. We are called the sandwich generation, squeezed between raising teenagers and caring for declining parents. Increasingly, from the perimeter of our thoughts, the voice becomes clearer, more distinct, more frequent. The voice reminds us, "Strong, attractive, capable woman, you too will soon be old. All that you are doing for your own mama is a rehearsal for your own season." In the far distant horizon is the prospect of your own non-being.

I am a woman in mid-life. This is the season that all my friends are contemplating old age. Ours are the conversations that detail our fluctuating estrogens, fibroid masses and forfeited wombs. Aches multiply and we must be intentional not to mention them too much, too often, to the same persons, as we faintly remember our own grandmother's mantras. These are the hushed telephone calls for comfort and prayer before our biopsies, and yes, the search for sisters who have walked before us when we too get the bad news of various sorts. We are the women with expendable incomes who now purchase treadmills and gym memberships instead of another suit or dress. We are trying to stave off the telltale signs of cellulite, sagging midriffs or loose underarms. We spend a bit more time now at the mirror or the cosmetic counter, reflecting about whether to color our gray strands or to celebrate them. And we are the women who secretly appreciate a lingering glance from a young man in his 30's (or even 20's) simply because we are too often invisible to the men in our lives, or perhaps because the men in our lives have disappeared. We are the women who are having the conversations we remember coming out of our mothers' mouths ("Lord Chile, I used to change your diapers, and now you got a baby yourself!") We are the women who in just a moment will be old.

Unless, of course, disease interrupts the processional, and police-man-like, orders a detour, a shortcut that omits the geriatrics from the itinerary. Breast cancer ... *again?*

This is the line up. Fall in. Like it or not, this may signal the death march. And next, you will be in line to be dead. Being the strong take-care-of-business black woman, one who never liked being bullied by a potential blackmailer, you do what you've always done. You make a decision.

The cancer could be back. It has been nine years and your radiographs have not changed. But look at this cluster of cells. His pencil encircles a luminous spot on the x-ray of my one remaining breast. My husband and I peer in the darkness to lock in on the enemy, and try to act all grown up.

The breast. The average person probably does not spend very much time contemplating its wonder. Then one day you must decide. Decide if you can live without it. Decide if disfigurement is worse than death. Decide how it will alter your marriage or your marriage-ability. Decisions. Decisions.

Breasts.

In pre-adolescence, we await their arrival with timid excitement. We supplement their tardiness in the mirror, with toilet tissue or balled-up-socks. We expose our progress in the girl's bathroom like versions of show and tell, and brag about brassiere purchases and exaggerated sizes. In college anatomy courses, we are awed by the graphs and charts: miles of highway ducts and fatty tissue and lobes. God's little kindness to combine the fluid of life with erotic pleasure, to bring comfort to our babies of whatever age. But by the time we are adult women, the breast settles comfortably into residence. In bathroom moments we occasionally size them up for firmness or sag, proportion or stretch marks and try to ascertain their delightsome quality to our most recent suitor. We monitor the cleavage depending on the context — "to see or not to see?" — that is the question. We lament shoulder grooves. We get reductions. We supplement the under-endowments. But mainly we just co-exist with our bosoms.

The breasts. In every society they are celebrated. Bare and exposed, they are adorned with mud and beads, henna paint and neck adornments. They are washed and perfumed and oiled and decorated in laces and satins. Suckled for nourishment. Caressed for comfort. Lain upon for solace. Tenderized to signal the hormonal escalations and declines throughout the month. Just part of who we are as women. The breasts. Intersection at which the maternal kisses the erotic, co-habiting as Siamese twins, connected in purpose and delight. Boobs. Titties. Jugs. Boulders. Melons. Mosquito bites. Whatever. They are yours.

It is outrageous betrayal when you discover that your breasts are out to kill you.

But as always, you make a decision. And decisions, like dots in the children's coloring book, connect to other decisions. Finally, you see a larger picture. On the back end of living, there is dying.

My life now is like frequenting an airport. Unknown travel date, but certain that *it is* scheduled. So I appear every day about the same time. I drive through and scan the crowd for arriving passengers. Being satisfied that she did not come on this flight, I proceed into my day. I will come again tomorrow though, just to check. Faithfully, I appear inside my life, wondering if this will be the day of death's arrival.

He is a stranger. I have an appointment to meet him. I just do not know what he looks like or even in what gender it travels. *It is appointed unto man once to die ...* we will meet, for the Bible assures me. But what will this stranger be like? I have no clue of the apparel she dons, or what her temperament will be that day. I have no idea of the stature in which she will present. Will he be gruff and coarse, mishandling me as we walk away? Will he seduce me: make me long for him at last, and run into his waiting arms? Will she be like an old familiar girlfriend, known intuitively, needing no words between us?

I just know I will recognize her when she is upon me. The eye contact maybe. Or the sure-footed gait in my direction. Death. The one certain end. All else is a preparation for this grand finale. And she will come for me again, and the next time perhaps, I will not resist her.

My closest friends say I have an ongoing "dialogue with death." But honestly, I do not spend excessive hours peering into my own grave. It would render one morose, melancholy and I am not; I am genuinely happy with my life. Yet when one's life has been perched so precariously on the grave's edge, there is a consciousness of dying which becomes familiar. Inescapable. A part of where you live: like the tree outside your window or a chair in the room, seldom sat in, camouflaged by gathering stuff, but now a part of the permanent landscape.

Death will come for me. Breast cancer has intruded upon my privileged ignorance. I cannot pretend that death is only for others, the old, the infirm, for the elders of my life. She has brushed past me, and I have felt the texture of her garments. Maybe next time, I will not resist her.

For those who may outlast me and be left to do the sorting out of my stuff and the discovery of my post-mortem secrets, I am moved to submit my final will and testament concerning my exit. I suspect that my breast is out to kill me.

Do not forbid me to remain dead.

I shall have done the painful pre-flight work of disconnecting the emotions, dislodging the long lain roots in the substance that was life. I will have opened my hand from the grip that "owned" my lovers, and my memories. My future will be mourned. My loved children handed back. My things that will hold my scent for awhile after I am gone will be parceled out or left aside.

And excruciating it will all be.

Cancer, one time, makes you do a dress rehearsal, even down to the last curtain call.

Cancer, a second time, releases the adrenaline, and that sick queasy feeling of being called to take center stage in just a very few minutes, knowing that this part has no supporting cast. And you find the courage to make decisions.

When the stranger comes for me, I know I shall protest. But maybe next time not too, too much. I think it may be the sense of relief. "Aha, so this is she." She, who teased me and bullied me from the other side of the known. She will be my final escort. My final companion, who shall release me to God.

Grave where is your victory? Death where is your sting?

The last enemy that shall be destroyed is death.

Indeed. For after death's final blow, there is *nothing else she can do*. She shall be destroyed; never again shall she intrude into the affairs or the domain of God's own.

So please, do not forbid me to remain dead.

If I should land in the hands of well meaning medical magicians who, like Buckingham guards, stand over my waning breaths and count them down like commodities, YOU protect me from their intentions. Once my spirit has chosen the exiting breath to ride upon from my earthly house, in all sense of duty and unreflective zeal, they will forbid me to remain

dead. Lest they stuff my or their breath back into my wea-
ried lungs, please speak on my behalf. Tell them what I said
when my lips were not sealed by age or suffering. Be my
voice, when I am on the brink of my demise.

If I am still in the hands of the faithful, those who will hold
me because of their own collective influence with God, tell
them to adjourn the prayer meeting, and turn it into a time of
worship. Their prayers have mighty weight with God, and just
perchance, they may want me to remain; just perhaps by
their prayers and supplications to the throne of God, the
saints would presume to hold my soul in this life, tell them for
me, to *cease.* My decision long, long ago, has been to go with
God.

*

A dialogue about death and a dialogue about breasts are
bridged by the diagnosis of cancer, and the prospect of its
recurrence. This time it was not my mother or my grandmother. This time it was potentially me. Having breast cancer, or any catastrophic illness despite its stage or severity is
a wake-up call about living fully and dying well. It is to grasp
the resolve that no, dying is not necessarily the worst thing
that can happen. *It is the "not living" that should make us cry.*

It is a wake-up call to make decisions you pretend you will
never have to make, at least not now. "If the cancer is back...?"
Though it is the basic human instinct to cling to life until its
very essence yields ... now one ponders: "What would I do,
what decision do I make?" Would I enter again the uncertain,
cruel covenant with the chemicals? The scalpel? The
catheter? Decisions. Would I tell my Mama again, and could

she stand it? Would my husband have any more to give?

And then there are the housekeeping issues we all wish to defer. Do you have a will? Where do you wish to be buried? Who will preach your funeral? And what will be the testimony about your life, for those friends and onlookers who might attend? Will you have finished your assignment on the earth? Who haven't you been able to forgive? Who will you be estranged from when you close your eyes? Will you have loved anyone well enough and thoroughly enough, that your disappearance will rend their heart and leave a missing space in their real life?

What will be the condition of my death, or yours? Will it be swift and ambushing, suddenly, without announcement? Or will it be a slow journey home, long and protracted? Alas, how will the stranger finally appear? When these decisions are shoved into one's face like so many smelling salts, to jolt me from my fantasies of permanence, I make a decision.

And the decision is made.

Do not forbid me to remain dead. Life has been a privilege!! I have been divinely, providentially favored amid all my complaints and comparisons! I have loved living! I have been loved by life and a few incredibly wonderful people. Say goodbye, lean your head upon some remaining breast and cry deep and soul- emptying cries if you loved me.

But then, do not cry too long.

It was like heaven being here with you.

And now, on to the real thing!

*Keep me as the apple of Thine eye, hide
me under the shadow of thy wings ...from
the wicked...and from my deadly enemies...*

Psalm Seventeen

*

She knew the *day* the marriage was over. Long
before the children told her about the other
women; long before the harsh words; or the
secrets. It was the way he *stopped looking* at her.
Started looking past her. Looking through her
like she was some kind of windowpane.

*

*"May God give you the spirit of wisdom
and revelation in the knowledge of Him,
and may the eyes of your understanding be
enlightened to know your hope..."*

Ephesians Chapter Three

Chapter Four
On The Meeting Of Eyes

Redemption On The Outside Aisle

It was a dusty, sweltering September day in Texas. The kind that burns your bare feet when they touch the concrete, or makes you jump when your thighs presume to rest on the metal chair in the backyard. We were at the Marlin Women's Correctional Unit. Barbed wire decorated the perimeters. Concrete floors. Bars on every window. Stark. Forbidding. The kind of hot that dares you to breathe. One big old aluminum fan circulated the oven-air as we entered. Not a place you would leave your beloved dog. Comfortless. Part of our women's outreach to touch so-called women offenders. Extortionists, thieves, addicts, drug related criminals, armed robbers, sexual deviants, killers. Offenders.

There was the inevitable. The sizing up. The split-second evaluations that women do. Women on "their" side had already learned to survive by all the "cons" and could sense if they themselves were being set up for one. It was the message, the look that said not to come with any of the bull. *Who is this and what is she coming with?* There were the decisions, the pseudo-Christian evaluations on my side. *How sophisticated are they? What will they hear ... what can they understand? How do I perform; do I try a bit harder than normal to prove my credibility?*

From somewhere within me I am instructed. *Just relax and*

do what you do.

Lord help me. Okay. The other takes too much work.

Yet somehow, as I preached in the midst of the sea of white uniformed women, I saw my aunts, my nieces, my sister, even my grandmother. Our eyes met. Our knowing somehow forgave our differences in choices and in circumstances. In all their offense and offensiveness, they were somehow familiar. In all my religion and my roles, I was somehow trustworthy.

And there she was. In my peripheral vision, over to the left nearest the aisle, there was another kind of woman — one outside the repertoire of my familiarity. Unwelcoming. Unyielding to my charm, my charisma or my Christ.

All over the room I saw hands raised in surrender; in pain and in gratitude for genuine redemption. I witnessed tears rendezvous beneath the chins of worshiping women — offenders — yielding to a Hope. *May these words from this lady preacher touch the rotting places in my life.* There was a decay which had begun to fester, long years ago. But the decay could not rot out the Hope.

"For what we see, why do we yet hope for..."

(Romans 8:24)

Then I spied the woman, on the left nearest the aisle. Her thick muscular arms were folded solidly across her broad chest. Her neck short, thick. Her hair cropped close to her head. Her leg crossed, ankle across knee. Her gaze went straight through me. Not glaring, not enraged. That would have signified some "life force" behind those eyes. She sat there, square, mannish, brutishly defending herself in dead-ness. Closed off against whatever remaining indignities life might still dare to bring. She looked straight through me, unseeing. Amazing how the soul's impressions are made in split seconds. "Eyes with no one behind them," I thought.

Our text today, my sisters, is taken from John 7:53-8:11: "A Good Woman in a Bad Situation." You know the story. The woman caught. Capital punishment looming. Her sentence is commuted by Jesus as He writes on the ground. And Jesus looks up from the writing, **and sees her** ... *mercy can prevail. Life can begin again.*

The Holy Spirit translated my words into the hearts and lives of women. The atmosphere changed. Charged. Electric with the anointing to set people free. The gray gloom of the Marlin Auditorium was pushed back by the Shekinah of God! And there she sat, the lady on the left, closest to the aisle. Arms folded, leg crossed, eyes unseeing. Daring me to make her feel God.

It is finished. The guards are winding us up. Our clock has expired. We are being hustled out. Forbidden the closure which attends these kinds of meetings; we cannot embrace the women, we cannot touch their faces or lay hands upon their needs or give respect to their tears. Maybe no one ever has.

That is the primal offense.

Nevertheless, *they* are tagged, "the offenders." "Do not touch them," we are sternly admonished, as a condition of our permission to come. And the exit parade begins, as they remain seated, forbidden to rise till the preacher and her team have gone. They cheer, they shout, they whistle; they keep on singing as we wave goodbye. I leave by the left side of the hot, gray dismal auditorium, on the path to the woman with the dead eyes and the folded arms. I am approaching her, but her bullishness makes me afraid to confront her with my eyes.

I have almost passed her.

From out of a hulking grave it seems, "someone" arises, from within her still seated body. Arises and comes up behind the dead flat eyes.

The eyes.

The only fleeting clue.

Not a demon.

Not an alien spirit.

Not an offensive presence at all. "Life is alive," said the mystic, Howard Thurman, and it recognizes and craves its own. She disregards the rules ... after all she is an offender, accustomed to choosing her own boundaries. That moment, as she grasps my passing hand — the lady on the left nearest the aisle — is a penitent child.

I am startled as I feel her tender, fleshy hand. Her hand on mine contradicts the steeliness she has wanted us to see. It confronts my unconscious revulsion, and demands, for just that instant, that I see her humanity. My eyes meet hers. Locked only for a second, but for me, and I think for her, it was an eternal transaction. In one look, I see her plead behind those tear-filled eyes. I see her beg, vulnerable as a desperate infant. Regressed, vulnerable, open wide.

And Jesus looked up and saw her...

She looks squarely into my eyes; piercing the din and commotion of our leave-taking, she mouths, "Preacher, pray for me. Don't forget me."

And I am hustled out. I am gone.

*

Today as I write I am surprised by the heaviness of my heart. I still feel smothered by my sorrow for the lady by the aisle on the left. I wanted to run back and kneel before her chair and listen to her story and know what pains stripped her. What or who had made her femininity a place of un-safety for her? What had taught her to cocoon herself into concrete and dare anything to live in her heart? What had made the lady with the pleading eyes and the soft hand think herself safe behind the bullish, man-like persona? Didn't she know that in this world bulls are slaughtered for sport, and that given the right context, the men that she imitates are, too, just as helpless?

But the only thing I had to leave her was the message of our eyes.

"Where are thine accusers, woman?" Certainly not I.

"Go, and sin no more."

I will remember her till I die.

It was what came up quite by surprise, that day behind the dead eyes.

On Being First

We are finally in Kisumu, Kenya in eastern Africa. Way outside Nairobi. We have planned a foray into the Masai Mara compound. We have ridden ten hours, from the Silicon Chip to the Stone Age in a day. I spot small red dots on the horizon, tucked into the beige haze of the Savannah plain. "The women." They were taking the cows for the days-and-days journey to graze or to market or to whatever. The red dot is the Masai woman; wrapped in traditional red, for they say the red protects them against the wild animals. What other protection does a Masai woman pray for as she communes in the dusty, lonely wilderness with her cows? I wonder.

The men in our party are looking for animals. Cheetah. Lions. Wildebeests. I am looking for *people*. I insist. We must seek a welcome among the tribes.

We have come upon a compound of ten encircled huts. They are ingeniously made of cow dung and mud, and thatched grass roofs. Masai warriors and old men are lazing around the gates of the compound under shade trees, sitting on the ground being important. Round-bellied toddlers and women — beautiful, fine- boned sisters — are doing what women and children have done in every society from time immemorial. They are busy, working, creating the thoughtful infrastructures that make life thoughtless for others. The women ease their own burdens, and heighten their meager joys, by *doing life together*, as women and children do. Sometimes with, or sometimes without the aid of their men. Doing daily life. I think for a moment how lonely life can be for the women across the world — urban, European or American, of a certain class and neighborhood. But too often, with no sisters in the midst of daily life to comb their hair or shell peas with on the back porch or to trade evening stories of the funny thing that happened today at the market. African sisters were doing daily life, each a part of the fabric of each other's reality.

The chief's son is an English-speaking, London-educated

professional, returned home. He has traded in his western suit for his return to a simpler way of life, he informs us, smiling, in that way that suggests an apology. In multicolored cloths and native attire, his British accent is an almost pleasant contradiction in the sweltering wilderness. He is our translator, our guide and our barter-man. "Just a small offering of money for me, and I can guarantee to gain you access. Of course, the chief is busy but I can assure you..."

The world is shrinking.

I learn that his father, the chief, has five wives. Hence the several huts in the compound. I bend low as I am invited into a random hut, my eyes acclimating to the darkness of the little space, with its cool cow-dung walls and the miniature sleeping areas. It is cluttered, lived in. I am reminded of a cellar, or a dungeon, or some other place of my childhood imagination where we played hide and seek on hot summer days. Into this small dank space I shrink myself to fit. Here, two "warriors" sit on the built-from-the-wall cot, and drink the wilderness version of beer. Hanging out. Idle. Being. Just chillin'...like young black brothers 4,000 miles away in New York City or Atlanta or Los Angeles. Probably they are no more than 15 or 16 years of age, but learning already the state of male privilege.

Each wife has her own hut, I am told, and a sleeping space for herself and her children. The chief visits each one as scheduled. A curious arrangement I think, as I stand outside again in the circle of huts. But then again, I think of the men I have known, back in New York, Atlanta, Los Angeles, and the women who have *waited their turn* on some elusive schedule, for their man's homecomings.

We are back in the center of the compound. I note that we are protected by 7 to 10-foot high masses of portable thorn bushes — a massive encirclement. "To keep out the wild animals at night," I am told. "We bring the cows into the middle of the compound at night so they too are protected." The cows are honored.

Too bad about the women.

The gaggle of ripe young teenaged girls stand in a circle at a respectful distance, sizing me up, giggling, fascinated with my clothing or my hair or something. Or maybe they are critiquing me, as teenaged girls are prone to do to older women. They are beautiful already, and at 12, 13, 14 years old they will soon be wives of some 30ish warrior who can offer cows to their parents in exchange for a bride.

I ask permission to greet the First Wife of this chief. The senior wife. The one he first loved and chose and lay with to make children. Maybe it is my western prejudice; or maybe it is my years of competition from women who would have displaced *me* as the *first* wife. I want to offer a gift and thank her for receiving us. We stand in the midst of buzzing flies and piles of cow dung and colorful Masai people, the hot African sun beating down upon my straightened, bare head. I am taking it all in, in wonder, in awe. I am making mental notes of the condition of the children, their health, the order amid the primal wildness, the African sun beating down, beating down, beating upon my head. *It is making me delirious,* I think. The wonder of it all! Here I am halfway around the world, experiencing the things I always hungrily absorbed on the

Discovery Channel. I am being introduced through the layers of tribal bureaucracy, and finally she appears. A beautiful woman, fine boned and bronze. Hair cropped so close to her head it appears that she has just left the beauty shop on 115th Street. Beaded neck, dazzling reds and lapis and white. Probably barely 35. She is a First Wife. But in what sense? In this culture, I think to myself, she is already an old, used-up woman.

Her eyes tell the story. Sad eyes. Large deep-set eyes, encircled with the kind of blackness that comes only from life and weariness, and the constancy of a weight that will not move. These are eyes that see everything, but with one arch of the eyebrows, signal that she can do little about *any*thing.

I notice that like most black women everywhere, she has a girlfriend with her.

The girlfriend is talking over us with furrowed brow and impatient hands, herding and handling the children who encircle the First Wife's knees. She is bolder and seems more readily bothered by things than the placid First Wife. Girlfriend, I learn, is interjecting through the interpreter that instead of just visiting and talking, we should give money to *help them with these children.* I extend my hand.

It was all so fast.

I see her eyes dismiss me, look past me, beyond me. Her eyes are radar that pick up danger behind my back. There appears from across the compound ... out of nowhere ... a young warrior ... a flurry of punches ... the awful sound of flesh hitting flesh ... a shout of unintelligible but understand-able words.

The First Wife falls solidly on the hard, packed red ground. Then in a flash she scrambles to her feet ... dusty, disheveled, skinned and bloody. The First Wife is rushing to re-gather the dignity she has lost, like so many pearls from a broken necklace, scattered over the courtyard. The First Wife with the black circles under her obsidian eyes. She runs behind a hut as though its shadow can cover her shame.

It is a momentary thing, probably unnoticed by anyone but myself. She looks up. Brushing herself off hurriedly, looking at herself, she looks at me, at herself, and again at me. Her eyes find a path directly into my soul.

It is the look *that dares me to see, and not know.*

In a second she reached across the oceans, the culture, the vast divide of our worlds. The First Wife has pulled me in as her confessor, her matron, her tale-bearer. Her eyes said, *"This is how it is. Here. And in the apartment next door to you, or with the woman at your job. This is how it is, with some mother's daughter or some daughter's mother. For some of us, this is how it is."* It was the story told by the eyes.

There is a humiliation that only a woman knows, in the face of another woman. It is the time your mama whipped your behind right in front of the house, while all your third grade playmates were watching your snot and tears. Mama's strap is deconstructing your legends of big-girl-ness before their very eyes. This story in the First Wife's eyes is all about the humiliation that only a woman knows, when spied by another woman. It is when you need her to believe that things are better than they are. When *you* need to be the one who decides time and place to unveil your own sorrows, and surely not have your skirts thrown over your head, and your private things uncovered against your own will.

"Why did he hit her?" I asked, stunned. Appalled.

"He thought she was bothering you," The chief's son replied, matter-of-factly as he chewed on a twig and spat on the ground.

Not her husband.

Not her son.

Not a relative. Not that being related would have made it more bearable.

Just a man.

He had the entitlement and the privilege of knocking the brains out of the Chief's First Wife.

He had the power to send her reeling, scurrying like a frightened insect behind the shadow of the nearest hut.

The meeting of eyes.

See me. Know.

But do not look too long.

Sometimes the greater mercy is too avert the eyes. To look away.

But the story is already out.

It escaped in the shadow, behind the hut, through the cloud of flies and red dust. Behind the well kept cows and the colored beads. The story got out.

It was in the eyes.

The Long Red Light

Sometimes the eyes are hungry.

The bland sameness of familiar sights and streets and

schedules makes the eyes search. For stimulation. For inter-ruptions from the boredom. The eyes, like two homing pigeons, flitter amid the urban clutter, amid the visual trash of signs and advertisements and come-ons and crowds.

I sat at the red light, fiddling with the fuzz on the radio, try-ing to decide if I had enough time, before arriving at my office, to finagle the compact disc from the back seat without spilling my coffee. Forget it. At the intersection of the Wal-Mart and the Exxon station, my eyes began a search. Something better. Something deeper. Something more. The Texas Hill Country lay on the horizon. Why not just keep straight, play hooky, and spend the day sitting by the lake or contemplating the beauty of the bluebonnets before they fade? I need something, *anything* other than another day sit-ting at a desk, listening to problems, trying to pull up answers to questions that won't yield to a quick fix. I am weary of ped-dling inspiration from a drying well.

This sure is a long red light.

I had seen her when I approached the intersection.

She stood there, big as day in the bright Texas sunshine. No shade tree to camouflage her. No girlfriend, no traveling part-ner. No man to protect her from God knows what. No way to hide. No distraction from her big ole' self. There was a woman, no longer able to be constrained by embarrassment. Homeless. Between addresses. Outdoors. There she was. Who could miss her, wide open, across the street from the Wal-Mart store? A cardboard sign, with the block letters badly, hurried-ly printed, was her stick-up weapon at the window. She placed under arrest the driver of any vehicle unlucky enough to be caught by the red light.

My windows were up. The air-conditioner blowing upon my freshly made-up face, I pretended to look in the rearview mirror to check my lipstick. Instead, my eyes made room for her inside my car.

"Traveling. Need Help. God Bless."

The eyes are hungry for something that is not plastic. Not neon. Not a come-on. I looked sideways, and nodded. Then I looked straight ahead.

Sometimes, the eyes have a mind of their own.

The light was still red.

She was still right there. I could touch her if I reached outside my car window.

Before my hand touched her, my eyes felt her.

Her pasty white arm was *mottled.* Little strawberry pools of blood beneath her skin reminded me of a Rorschach test I took somewhere in psychology class — the kind that dares you to recognize images inside the ink mass. *What does this blob look like to you, young lady?* Big prune-colored bruises the size of a fist made their way like a railroad track. Her shapely legs with the too-big calves had fresh scabs, and an ugly wound that needed attention. *At least cover it up so we don't have to look at it for God's sake.*

Her hair was thin, greasy. Her face had that too-red, too-puffy look of a woman who had drunk too much and eaten too little. And the flimsy little sandals reminded me of the slides that Big Mama used to piddle around the house in. Surely not meant to stand up to the Texas concrete. *You can see a lot when you really look.*

Then she looked at me, squarely, head on, without hesitation. There was an innocence in the eyes that dared me to ignore her.

She smiled. *I used to be pretty.*

Several of her teeth were gone. *Someone kissed this mouth once. Tenderly. Sweetly.* Her mouth bore the story of a recent battle that she had probably not won. *I was in love. At least for awhile.*

The clothes were just something to cover the flesh. Worn. Budweiser T-shirt and some old denim shorts. *I used to have dreams.*

But when she smiled, her *eyes still smiled.* A big, broad, life-ain't-gonna-get-me-down smile. Crinkly little lines around those eyes. Her piercing luminous gray eyes contradicted her condition. *Go on around me,* I waved the traffic. The light flashed green now, but I had to stay.

"Where you headed?" I asked.

"Trying to get home to Amarillo. My old man beat me up. Decided I had enough. Decided I am going home. Want to see my kids."

The light was red again.

"You're on the wrong highway, you know that, don't you? You need to get back to 35." I noticed she was traveling light. A tattered cloth bag, and what she had on her back.

"Any road can get you there when you know where you're goin'," she grinned.

She was looking past me, behind me, being sure not to miss any benevolent soul who would offer her money instead of conversation.

"You okay? It looks like you might need to see a doctor."

"Naw. I'll mend. If I can just get home ... see my kids ... that'll be medicine enough for me." Her voice was gravelly, tired. Like she had not one more thing left for life to take from her.

Then she looked at me again and there was *a transaction*. It was of more value than the few dollars she hoped to receive, or that I had intended to offer. I was driving a luxury car. She was hitching to Amarillo. I just kissed my husband good-bye over the plans for this evening's dinner and worship service. She just fled her angry old man — probably not ever given the legitimacy of license or love — without a clue where she would sleep tonight. I populated the ranks of the middle class privileged, the saved, the secure. My security had made me restless, bored, grasping the landscape for meaning. The lady with the gray eyes populated the street life; her rootless-ness had made her resolute, focused, sure of where her roads would lead her, and that God would go before her because to be sure, no one or nothing else could.

The lady at the intersection across from the Wal-Mart, with the long red light, handed me a gift.

When her eyes smiled, they twinkled a coded language. She had in her possession some things that maybe I had mis-placed.

The ability to never let your dreams die, no matter how wounded the dream may be.

The courage to leave, even if you have to travel by yourself.

The faith that someone will be compassionate. Merciful. Even strangers.

The strength to stand taller than your shame.

The internal compass to find your way back to love, even though you have been detoured by a thousand substitutes.

The "doing without" that sometimes leaves one richer in the end, than "the grasping" to hold onto everything.

I could send her to Amarillo for what I would spend on lunch that week.

"Well, can I drop you at the bus station?"

Are you crazy? You have appointments and this woman could be an ax murderer.

Sometimes the eyes are hungry for something that is not packaged, or painted. Not auditioning for your approval, or editing itself, concerned about your holier-than-me judgments. Sometimes the eyes are on a desperate search for connection, for meaning, for someplace to put a hand, a gentle touch.

On the other hand, there was the view from her eyes. The eyes seek someone to remind you that you are not invisible. They want, for some instant, to know that cringing and shrinking are not necessary; that one is welcomed and accepted regardless of one's traveling condition.

The eyes simply mirror what you both know — if anyone has the courage to translate.

"If your eye be single,
Your whole body shall be full of light," said Jesus.

I never quite understood that passage.

Until today. On the ride to the bus station.

Sometimes, the eyes tell it all.

The Crib in the Corner

It was a tossup.

What was worse? Was it the heat or the mosquitoes? Or was it the charcoal smoke, the dusty air, parching the throat and burning the eyes? Or was it the smells of rotting trash from the open sewer that kept the novices just on the verge of needing to vomit? Maybe it was the animal excrement just over the wall, or the unwashed human bodies? Or maybe it was the noise.

Today I think it is the noise. Noise, though it is an assault on the ears, can make the eyes blind to the moment's lessons.

The clamor was incredible.

It is the noise of *contrast* in Haiti. Some years, I visit the orphanages, and there is not this noise. When children are sick or hungry a long time, or just bruised beyond their years, there is a quiet about them. A weary quiet. They do not laugh; they do not run or play; they do not chat; they do not smile. They do not respond much to your touch. They just look. That piercing, look-through-your-soul look. The look puts you under arrest, and reminds you as an adult of your own complicity in their suffering. They just look. And their space is quiet.

But this day the clamor was incredible. It was the squeals and laughter and aggressive horseplay of healthy, excited children. From two years old, toddling around the room with saggy diapers, to the bigger children, nine, ten, eleven-year-olds, they were all in a state of randomness. Rowdy child's play. No toys, just each other. The workers stood back in their dingy white threadbare uniforms, absently overseeing the melee. They too had that Haiti-look. Overwhelmed. Tired. Doing-the-best-I-can-today-with-all-these-kids look. Even the room had that look. The cribs were peeling paint. The linoleum had seen its best days, curling at the corners, seams buckling, dirt that would not wash out. The sheets were long, long ago expired; gray and stained and ripped; barely adhering to the flimsy row of mattresses. *"Where is Martha Stewart when she is really needed," I think.* As many years as I have stood in this room, it still reminds me of a dormitory in what must have been a Russian or Hungarian or Polish war barracks for hungry, hardened men; or a Jewish concentration camp waiting point, from some 1940's black and white movie. Not a place for little children to live and grow up. But live, and grow up, they do. The children used the beds as a playground, jumping, leaping, playing their version of "king of the hill," oblivious for the moment of the warfare that is against them ever growing old.

The workers smiled politely at us, the visiting American missionaries, as if to say, "If you can do something with them, help yourself."

I trained the American missionaries to *look.* Not to go into Haiti skimming the surface, immersing in busy-work and missing the message. Not to go into Haiti, looking the other way. I chatted with one of the first-time missionaries as we surveyed our surroundings. She choked, swallowing the emotion of it all. "And I give away crib sheets because there is a carrot stain that won't come out; I throw away towels and baby clothes that would be like a Christmas gift to these children." I only nodded. She was beginning to *see* the ways in which privilege makes us sleepy, blind, and unconscious to the rest of the world.

We could hardly hear, but I prayed for them to *see*.

When there are no parents, no one-on-one mothering or fathering, children in group living must supplement their hunger for connection. They do so with one another. They fill the empty place that needs contact with their peers. They create their own dyads and triads, their own systems for protection and for power. There already are the young bullies; and those who must figure ways to outwit them. They create their own comforters and their own targets; they choose whom they will torment, and whom they will protect. They find alliances with each other, two or three children, here and there. These children need to touch hands and be held cheek-to-cheek and be rocked to sleep. They need a lap to sit on, or someplace human to lay their heads. They need some person with whom they can feel ... special. Exclusive. So these children forge a hand-done, make-do sense of family. It is a roughly-hewn, poor imitation of the stuff that — if the world was fair — should have been bequeathed by the nurture and attention of a mama and daddy of their very own.

In order to grow well and solidly, children must believe that they have value. It is their sense of anchoring in the world. Value is transmitted to a child's soul when she sees her mama smile a smile that is just for her. It is the child knowing that she can elicit the approval of her mama; the look, the attention, the curiosity that is just about her. It is the sense of confidence and worth that a child begins to claim as his own, when he sees himself reflected in his daddy's eyes. And it is the stuff that leaves a child forever needy and a bit uncertain, when she has not had the gift of *loving eyes*.

The little kids and the bigger kids, the clowns and the bullies, the charmers, the con artists and the wallflowers were all before me this hot noisy day in Haiti. This is life in the orphanage.

I do not know how many days I passed through this room. Two, three, five days? I went about the business of holding babies, clearing away dirty dishes, combing heads; hugging the most needing and demanding children and trying to draw out the ones who could not come and ask.

Then I saw *her*.

The child was in the crib, in the left corner of the room, right by the window. She lay there as though she had been placed out of the way. The child was alone, with her spindly little legs high in the air. For a moment, I thought of threads without the helium balloon on the end. Missing. Dancing strings, caught up in static electricity, standing alone in the air. But they were not baby legs. All the clamor and activity in the room kept a wide perimeter around this child. Not one worker or one child visited with her, looked upon her or touched her. Her fist was balled up and stuck awkwardly in her mouth, trying to suckle something from an unyielding life. She lay there in the crib in the corner, enveloped in her own aloneness, waving her little legs like a highway sign. "Can anyone see me over here?" "LOOK!" "Look at me! Hey, you over there, hey! HEY!!"

I went to her and picked her up. She was light, like a feather almost. She was small, but strangely I knew she was not a baby. Arms and legs were too long and well formed; too many teeth crowded into her small mouth. Through my halting Creole and the response of the ill-informed women "workers," all I learned was that her name was Bernadette and she was about seven years old. No one was sure if she could hear, or if she was mentally retarded, or if she could see. Little Bernadette was the size of a small three year old; her skull was shrunken, malformed. Her caramel colored skin was beautiful, lacking only touch, caress, stroking and maybe a little lotion.

In Haiti, one is always engaged in an internal dialogue between safety and sacrificial love. Is the child diseased? Does she have parasites or impetigo or AIDS? When I hold her close to my face and speak loving words into her ears, will I breathe in tubercular marauders looking for a home in my lungs? Nonetheless, the child in the crib in the corner, who could not speak, kept calling my name.

Legs. Skin. The black old scar her teeth had left on her fist. Cranial shape. Pretty little feet. Crowded teeth. Cottony little bit of dull hair, sandy, uncombed.

But it was the eyes that drew me in.

Bernadette could not speak and I know not if she could hear. But she had *eyes that shouted* at me, if I cared to listen. When she lay alone in her little metal prison, trying to comfort herself, her eyes simply rolled up into some corner of the crib. Her eyes darted nervous little movements, too quick to count. Searching for something. Anything to verify that she was in the world.

But when I drew the child close to my breast, I watched her

eyes.

I tipped across the bridge, the chasm of her isolated existence.

I whispered love into her ears, warm, near.

I held her close and tight, and rocked her so she would not have to rock herself.

Bernadette's contortions stopped and her flailing legs relaxed upon my body.

And her eyeballs stopped the frantic search.

Her eyes listened, though they could not make out a form.

Bernadette was in my arms. Valued if only for a moment. Eliciting a smile that she could never behold. I held the child and I did not want to let her go.

Her eyes *held me* in return, though her arms — too weak and disconnected from her brain—-could not return the embrace.

Her eyes relaxed.

Her eyes held a gaze in the direction of my voice.

Her eyes surrendered to the soft, safe place that every person deserves: The expectation to be sweetly, indulgently cherished.

Mama?

The little girl's eyes bugged as she peered
through the dark house, pulling her
playmate along by the hand.
"Ain't you scared?" hissed her
tiny companion.
"Sho' is!" she whispered back, still
creeping. "But you jus' hold my hand and
keep walkin' where I walk. Might as well
come on ... we done come this far ... and
we both in trouble now anyway."

*

Jesus said, "If you go, I'll go with you.
Open up your mouth and I'll speak
for you."
"Lord if I go, tell me what to say.
They won't believe in me."

Traditional Gospel Song

Chapter Five
Gateways

I spend a great deal of time contemplating gateways.

I am the product of a generation of women who dared to question some closed systems: "How do I get into the places that have denied me access?" And "who said" I do not belong? I was formed from a family and a social climate (albeit, not in the Christian community) that taught me to question the places which erected "keep out" signs because of my color (as a child) or my gender (as an adult). The generation of women formed in the last half of the 20th century went beyond what we were told we could, or could not do. As unapologetic Christians, we dared to investigate for ourselves the texts of Holy Scripture, in light of culture and ancient custom. We are the group who were reviled from the pulpits of men, made to preach from the floor, made the brunt of unkind female humor and often, gender innuendo, and were expected to nod, smile, look straight ahead and be "good sports." All the while we were thinking, "How am I going to get beyond this reality?" Silence does not mean consent.

Gateways: Which one is the right one? We are the women who too often had to make choices, to be loved by men and be married *or* to be smart, assertive, creative, thinking women — but not both.

I am a part of a generation of women bred in the last quarter of the 20th century, upon whom the Spirit of the Lord fell, and who went forth as the "prophesying daughters" of Joel 2:28 and Acts 2:17. We stand on the shoulders of our spiritual mothers, who began to chisel tiny cracks in the ecclesiastical closed systems from the 1700's on: Jarena Lee amid the African Methodists; Nannie Helen Burroughs faced the National Baptists in 1901; Ida B. Robinson among the Pentecostals who rose up and founded an entire denomination which flourished during the years of the American Depression; Bishop Ernestine Cleveland Reems among the Church of God in Christ, who became the first major pioneering pastor in the 1950's, leading the way despite hostility and ostracism. Women like the Reverend Johnnie Coleman in Chicago amassed multi-million dollar empires preaching healing and prosperity, eclipsing any existing institutions of that kind. Bishops Leontine Kelly and Barbara Harris among the United Methodists and the Anglicans, respectively, were among the first to open the American Episcopacy as women Bishops. Dr. Ella Mitchell, one of the first pastor/scholars, became a writing force for the controversial cause of women preachers with her multi-volumes on <u>Those Preaching Women</u>[2]. These women and countless others[3] saw gateways, and sometimes dared to create them where none was visible. They believed that God-ordained opportunities were permission enough to get them moving. As educator and scholar Dr. Renita J. Weems quotes often, "Well-behaved women seldom make history!"

---

[2] Mitchell, Ella Pearson. THOSE PREACHING WOMEN, Volumes 1-3. Valley Forge, PA: Judson Press 1996

[3] See Ruth Tucker and Walter Liefield. DAUGHTERS OF THE CHURCH: Women in Ministry from New Testament Times to the Present. Grand Rapids: Zondervan, 1987

Women of every age and color have defied the norms of exclusion and injustice. Deborah saw a political opportunity when there was a vacuum of sound leadership, and became a Judge in Israel. "Village life had ceased until I, Deborah, arose as a Mother in Zion," she sings in Judges 5:7. Though it was on the back of Vashti's unfortunate firing as the queen, Esther saw a gateway to use her feminine influence to save the nation of the Jews. Mary, the mother of Jesus, has been marginalized in Protestant Christianity; yet she *became* a gateway as she carried in her body the Light that would come into the world and change salvation-history for all eternity. Women like Ida B. Wells fermented the anti-lynching movement in the American south; Susan B. Anthony and her peers fought for a woman's right to vote. Rosa Parks got tired of sitting on the back of segregated buses, and roused the sleeping south. Martha Stewart believed she could build her own corporate empire, and get paid by the same rules the good old boys did; Hillary Clinton became a modern illustration, that if a woman could use her intelligence, political know-how and savvy to put her husband in the highest political office in the land, she could use that same political capital for herself, too.

And these are the courageous women *whom we love to hate.*

In the prophetic spirit of every age, strong women have defied the norms. These women have been hated, maligned, and openly despised by other women who thought we "did not know our place" or were "trying to be men." Our real crime was that we believed the *gift of God* was not given by mistake, nor because "a man refused the gift" nor with "respect of persons," or gender or color or class. That kind of audacity will get you hated.

There are women even today who would exclude powerful women from their Christian circles. Churchwomen will be blessed, delivered and set free, feeding from my own ministry, listening to my tapes, and buying my books. Yet in conversation, depending on the context, they will damn me to hell for saying "yes" to the full definition of myself as a preacher/pastor. There is a kind of unspoken disdain for "women like me" who (they say) exhibit insufficient subordination to my brothers, and are just a bit too different from all the regular sisters they know. No, they would never choose me for a friend — yet they now walk unobstructed — or for sure, *watch their daughters walk through the gateways* that my "mothers" and women of my generation opened wide. College education is a given. They enjoy equal pay for equal work, and they are welcomed into corporate boardrooms or military ranks; they have the choice to *not have* children, stay at home *with* their children or to own and administrate entire educational systems *for* children; they mount pulpits or judges' benches or airplane cockpits. They can be construction workers or architects — because some woman contemplated and took advantage of a gateway, and its meaning *for larger life.*

Stuck? Frustrated with your level of living? Wondering if God has cheated you, because of the present barrenness of your life? The issue is not the lack of avenues, doors, thresholds or opportunities. The deception is in your failure to see them, look for them, think about how God presents them. All around you, every single day, God presents gateways.

I have spent much of my life thinking about gateways. I

know they are seldom passed through without significant emotional distress. There is inevitable fear of the future, grieving those you may have to leave behind, or anxiety about the unknown. Whatever. That's the price of the ticket. But you must keep on coming!

It Swings Both Ways on the Hinges

I have studied and mulled over how to get into spaces and places. As importantly, gateways demand a working knowledge of how to get *out of* others. Ideologies at one season of life can be inspirational, and at another season can become crippling. For example, there is one season to get into a church community. In another season, in spite of loyalties and history, it may be mandatory to get out, or turn to a pillar of salt — ossified like a fossil. Lot's wife. Systems that once nourished us can become mean or toxic. You can outgrow a job that you once saw as a Godsend. Ideas can expire; you must learn new facts as fodder for new territory. Relationships we once relished can turn on us; you must learn to see what you are now seeing, hear what you are now hearing, in light of "now" and not *"what was."*

People. Relationships. Situations. If it walks like a duck, and quacks like a duck, and swims like a duck, do you still need to believe it is the eagle it used to be? "What a fool believes, she sees," said one songwriter. "What a person won't believe, she will never see," said the Bible.

Gateways: How do you get out of the places which are suffocating, or stifling to growth, or places which have begun simply boring you to death? How does a woman get out, when she is afraid to make folks mad at her, or has been taught she must not hurt anyone's feelings by leaving, or when the notion of walking alone paralyzes her? She whines. She complains. She pisses and moans about the people who are causing her grief and sorrow. She feels that she is the eternal victim. She sees what every other person should be doing, to ameliorate her suffering. She clings to God and Scripture to validate her imprisonment. She does everything she can to pretend that the gateway does not exist.

In my childhood, gateways signaled a welcome to come and play when they were open. I presumed I was invited. Gateways meant danger, when they incarcerated "King," the local bad dog. I knew from shared childhood fables that King would eat you alive if you got too close. I learned which nighttime closed doors I had to knock on and wait, lest there be embarrassment and scurrying for cover. Then there were the closed doors I could always walk through and be automatically welcomed, jump up on the bed and find a morning kiss and a hug. Every little girl learns how to read gateways early in life.

The problem arises when she becomes a woman, and is talked out of knowing what she knows.

In airports I am weekly walking toward a gateway, waiting outside one, or reading an electronic screen in search of the right one.

As a menopausal woman, I am figuring out this physical gateway to the next season of life: what pleasures and unrestrictions I have to look forward to. I watch the teenaged daughters of my life approaching the gateways to woman-

pleasures and pains, and tremble in prayer that they will not be devoured before they step through the portal. Visiting a prison recently, I was escorted beyond areas of barbed wire and metal enclosures. How profoundly symbolic a gateway becomes depending on which side of it you stand! The gateways are barriers to escape or guarantees of freedom and a future. They are safety or suffocation.

The problem is that gateways are often camouflaged.

They are packaged as *days*: You presume you have tomorrow so you sit still, just one more day. Today you should apply to school. Today you should enroll and take one course. Today you should begin to exercise, stop smoking, drink more water, walk around the block, or walk away from the violence. Today you should trust your heart and give yourself again to love. Marry him! Today, you should put *him* out, realizing that he is never, ever going to commit *to you*. Whether it is your education, a new business, your health, an address change or a life change; whether it is a choice to start saving a few dollars, or a chance at love, all are at the fingertips of this day. One day you will wake up and realize that more days are behind you than in front. You will realize with sickening certainty how you have let the "gateways" slip through your fingers ... because, well, there was always another day. "Lord, teach us to number our days," one writer prayed, "so that we may apply our hearts to wisdom."

Gateways.

They are camouflaged as *decisions*: You won't risk disapproval, so you silence the voice shouting from inside your "knower." The relationship has long ago expired. But you do not have the courage to make a decision; you are scared to be alone; you have rationalized the violence, the humiliation, the being ignored, so by default, a decision is made for you. You have outgrown the job, but the illusion of security keeps you in a small space, while vision inside you grows fainter each passing year. You blame others; you protest that you "cannot do it with these kids." But still you hear the nudging: "Make the move; jump in; just do it." Every day you drive past the needs, the hunger, the ignorance, the kids who need a mentor. Instead of making a decision, you make an excuse. "I am going to pray about it," you declare. *And that ends that.* The gateway to a larger, fuller life begins to close because you feared the greatest gift God ever gave humans — the power to choose.

Once you make the decision and start walking, you will be surprised at how quickly people who oppose you now will "get over it." Your news soon becomes old news, and in a month or a year, "they" have found some other woman to discuss, to judge or to talk about over coffee. You will be amazed at all those years you wasted, waiting for approval or permission. It was not "the people" you had to protect, or who held you back or had any real power to stop your destiny. It was all in a decision.

Or gateways are packaged as *dilemmas.*

Di-lemma: Two competing options, which look equally valid, or equally dangerous. Dilemma: The paralysis of analysis. As a child I learned a valuable lesson from a cockroach as she eluded my murderous intentions. As I meandered into

99

my grandmother's kitchen in the middle of a hot southern night for a glass of water, she, the roach, was caught in a flood of light she did not expect. She wanted to eat, but she also wanted to live. Headed for the tasty crumbs to satisfy her appetite but — was it worth the cost of her life? Exposed!! The center of all my attention. No place to hide. Dilemma: Rather than stick around to negotiate with me about her appetite for the evening's leftovers, over against her chances of survival, she scurried through a crack.

I had never noticed it.

I would never have seen it.

But then again, I did not need it. *Her dilemma revealed her options.* Like the cockroach in Big Mama's kitchen, you too are in a dilemma. The spotlight is on you. You have hidden as long as you could. And you have no more time to negotiate. Praise the Lord!! Maybe now you will see, with Pharaoh on your heels and the whole Red Sea inviting you to drown — you'd better do something with what is already in your bag of possibilities.

In liturgy, the "hymn" was historically the "gateway" to the life-giving Word or Eucharist. It derives from the same Latin word "Hymen" — gateway to the womb. It protects against the intruders. But that gateway must be passed, however painfully, before passion can be experienced, or life given.

In your personal relationship, is there a "gateway" that begs for a decision? Is your mind stagnant — outside an educational door you will not enter? Call today and get the catalogue, and fill out the application. Is there a dream you keep nesting and nursing, not giving life to it because it will "hurt to do it?"

Get your research started. Who needs this idea? Where can you find a building or should you work from home? *So what* that it has never been done. Maybe God has reserved a space in history with your name on it. Have you been called to a door of ministry, to a foreign field, or to an all-too-familiar need that nags and irritates you each time you see it? Do you wonder why shopping feels shallow and eating is not nourishing the hunger? Maybe while you watch and wonder about every other anointed, competent woman ... your "yes" could be the gateway to your very purpose in life.

There is a pain worse than breaking through the gate.

It is dying on this side of it. You say you do not have a key? Try the knob. It just may be unlocked already.

Learn from the cockroach. *Now scurry!*

There are those who are willing
To die for Christ.
Never confuse this with those
Who end up
Dead
From
Christianity.

*

I know your works and your labor and
your patience ... and for my name's sake
you have not fainted.
Nevertheless I have this against you.
You no longer love Me
Like you used to love Me.

Jesus to the church at Ephesus, Revelation Chapter Two

Chapter Six
In Love With My Neighbor

"Ye who do earnestly and heartily repent of your sins
And who are in love and harmony with your neighbor,
And who do intend to lead a new life,
Draw near, with full assurance of faith..."
(Book of Common Prayer)

I do not love my neighbor.

Not as I should.

Not in a way that translates well.

Not as I wish.

I do not *see* my neighbor.

I do not know who my neighbor really is.

I cannot reach my neighbor, across the miles and miles of our differing interests and our conflicting schedules.

I tire of my neighbor's needs and expectations of me, because I am a professing and professional Christian.

I cannot trust enough to *come close* to my neighbor, try as I might, simply because of my history with other neighbors in my long gone past.

I am ashamed.

I do not love my neighbor as I ought. I am not in love with my neighbor.

But the miracle is that I still want to be.

On the other hand, I *do* love my neighbor.

I love my neighbor. I get up in the wee hours of the night to answer my neighbor's call.

I love my neighbor. I am amazed at the access my neighbor has to my caves, invading my night rest with their faces and unknown signals.

I love my neighbor. How readily I know his distress. How loudly I hear her cry. Across the midnights, across the miles.

I love my neighbor. She camps out on my heart, like a squatter.

I love my neighbor. My hand is open. My door is ajar.

I spent my life to study so I could serve him with integrity.

I ignored my vacations and my own liberties, to be present at my neighbor's funerals or weddings or their child's crisis.

I close my mouth to my own human pettiness and irritation at my neighbors unkindness toward me; rather I pause, ready to consider her story, her pain, and I pretend to myself that she does not injure me — well, not all that much.

I love my neighbor, who when needing the refuge of our home, it becomes my central joy to serve.

I do love my neighbor. My marriage took a back seat to my neighbor's relentless needs.

I do, really, un-resentfully love my neighbor.

My neighbor probably does not have a clue.

Ergo. Could it be...?

I do not love my neighbor.

I am not in love with my neighbor.

The miracle is that I do still, desperately, want to be.

The Question For Love

I have a secret selfish thought. It is not the question of spiritual, self-sacrificing Christian women. It smacks of a dangerous, bothersome presumption: that a *woman matters*, and deserves at least as much attention and yes, love as she has been willing to give to all those "suckers" and "takers" in her space.

Maybe it is not really a proposition for "real Christians" as you define the term. It is a subversive question but it persists. *"Have I, have you been well-enough loved?"* For you see, the possibility of being in love and harmony with my neighbor must be in some way connected by this underground cable, with this obscure question. *"Have I been supplied with what I need to give away what I must?"*

> *"I have tended my brothers' vineyards,*
> *But my own vineyards I have not kept."*
> (Song of Songs)

How is it that I can give what I have not received in good measure? From God you say? From the power of the Holy Ghost, you intone? As an act of my sanctified will, you admonish? True. True. But maybe not the whole truth.

Love must have a prevailing human space in which to exist with honor.

> *"Giving honor to God, Who is the head of my life*
> *My Lord and Savior Jesus Christ,*
> *Giving honor*

*To my pastor and honor to all the saints
and friends..."*

Such was the public litany of my formative life in the
church. This was the kind of prologue by which we were
taught to present ourselves when speaking publicly on any
occasion. We were taught to give honor to that which is
Divine, and those in divinely ordained positions. Every person knew it with rehearsed precision. We were trained to
honor the "love we give," to be true to it, to dress it appropri-
ately, to keep it warm and responsive with a smiley face
painted on it.

We were not tutored in being *loved well*. How do women
learn to give honor to the love we need? "Giving honor to
myself..." Jesus put it this way: "Thou shall love the Lord thy
God, with all thy mind, and all thy soul and all thy strength,
and thy neighbor as thyself." *As thyself. As thyself.*

The Climate for Love

Love creates a climate for all things. Yet it also deserves an
atmosphere no less than your child, or your pet, or your
African violet. A climate in which love itself can flourish.
Love does not just make an atmosphere; love *itself craves* an
atmosphere, a human environment which is friendly to the
notion of love, which respects its right to exist, and which
believes the lover to be necessary. With all our Christian rhetoric, love does not stay well where it is not cherished and
watered. Love must be personalized; she needs to have her

name called out loud in recognition. "You love me, and I see it." Love must climb upon a certain skeleton, to give itself form. Love must have a surrounding substance that is hungry *for It* — hungry for *my* specific love, in order to flourish. In essence, love expresses itself best when it has a place to go.

Oh, I know, *I know*. We Christian women have learned well the art of loving those persons, and in those spaces, which do not love us in return.

> *If you love those who love you,*
>
> *What thank have ye...?*
>
> *For even sinners do the same.*
>
> *(St. Matthew)*

We are masters of excusing or chasing our absent daddies; sustaining ambivalent or apathetic men; supporting selfish, thoughtless children far into the age of chronic immaturity. I am sure that Jesus knew we would have to love some people *in self-defense*. We know how to decorate the atmosphere of churches or friendships that do not feed our love in return. "Good theology," we have been told. "Unsatisfying living," we want to say in reply. We have been trained to provide enough love for ourselves and everyone else at the table. Mold. Meld. Fit. Stay. Pray. Mediate. Interpret. We have trained ourselves *not to need* to breathe deeply in a loving atmosphere. Just take little sips of air, and make it suffice. In Jesus' Name. Amen. Then we reach a time when more years are gone than are ahead of us, and terms like "resentment" or "cheated" or "what-the-heck-have-I-been-doing?" begin to claw at the out-skirts of our hearts. We wake up one day and the question floats to the surface of our half-used-up lives. "Have I been well-enough loved?"

> *"Love your enemies, and them which despitefully*
> *Use you."*

Okay, I think I got that one.

Have I wasted too much of my love in ground that could not yield an increase?

As I live out the latter half of my life, I have made an incredibly sobering discovery: I need to *envision another use* for my love. Scandalous thought! Can you imagine? Love in an atmosphere where my neighbor — whatever name or kin — brings *me* respect and affection, reciprocity and attention to sweeten *my* air? Christian women know how to be needed; we know how to be depended upon and at times, used; we know how to be approved of. How many women, beneath our proper roles, know what it means to be loved in our own houses, in God's house, in the houses of our friends?

Love's atmosphere becomes dreary without attention. Women become pale and anemic when we function too long, emotionally leaking or hemorrhaging as the case may be, and never asking the difficult questions. Who loves me in particular? And how am I being loved?

Love in the House of God

Love needs a welcoming reception that honors its gifts, its offerings, its coming.

As importantly, love burns low without a place to feed *from*.

For years, we have presumed that the holy church of God would foster that environment of love. If one did not have a man, she had her church. If one did not have children, she had her church. If one had no family, she made the church folks her kin. If one had no paying job, she had her church position to assign her worth. *And in each instance, that woman is looking for some type of love.*

We have ignored the reality that the holy Church is comprised of broken individuals who so much need the very love we/they have been tasked to produce upon demand. We have believed, without much proof, that the communion of the saints should sustain that atmosphere. We brought our transferred dreams to the church, of a father (pastor) who would re-parent us; a mother who would re-nourish us; sisters and brothers who would play with us and support us, maybe even admire us. We envisioned a holy family that would include "us" in their real lives.

And some have gone away disappointed.

When I was a young girl, I gave my heart and my love unquestioningly to the life of my local Sanctified Church. As a zealous adolescent "Junior Missionary," I looked forward to our annual congregational outings to the "State Meetings." Here we fellowshipped, ate, sang, cross-pollinated congregations, had a platform to show off our gifts, and indeed, to test the admiring waters of our small sanctified world. At 15 years old, I remember the day when I sensed that Christian love and kind encouragement could be a masquerade for "something other."

I remember Elder Joseph (the name is changed to protect

the guilty). He had shiny tight skin that always seemed too small for his pudgy, middle-aged body. He sat on the small platform around the pulpit with his too-small suit pants, legs gaping, and always in a state of semi-arousal, from the obvious outline in his pants. I can still see his receding gray hair, big teeth, and those huge moist lips, stretched tightly across them in a too-eager smile every time he saw me coming. "Love in the house of God." I can still recall the sickly feeling in my stomach when he came near, as I wrestled with "respecting my leaders" and protecting myself. I dared not tell my Bishop or my Youth Pastor. Who wants to be a troublemaker? I had no father, uncle or older brother in the church. So I ran to the refuge of the older women in the church, and praised the God of heaven for the knowing embrace of these "mothers" every time this man was in my space.

At 15, I was learning early to recognize the sickly courtship rituals of a pitiable man. His loveless existence had reduced him to "back door gestures" — probably long before he had ever come into the house of God. Or who knows, maybe he learned them there. Gestures of the flesh probably passed for love by his petty definition. A feel on my behind; a wet kiss on my lips if I were not fast enough in turning my head away during greeting time. The press of a few moist dollar bills into my hand under the guise of "encouragement." "Bless you daughter!" A crushing hold against my young breasts as he chanted, smiling, seemingly mesmerized by his intent. "Praise the Lord." He made a beeline for me in the parking lot, or in the church dining hall, when there were no chaperoning eyes. I knew the day. I marked it in my mind. I would always have to run from Elder Joseph, who probably came into the church legitimately hungry for love, and whose love-need turned him into a would-be predator.

We all expect "oxygen" from the church atmosphere. Instead there are times we get smoke and mirrors and illusions.

Which leaves us to define how and *if* love will continue to matter in the congregation of holy, damaged people. Can I be ... will I be ... is it safe to hope, that I may ever be truly "in love with my neighbor?"

I am now a pastor myself; thirty years later I am tasked with the manufacture, packaging and distribution of the same spiritual and emotional atmosphere that meets the needs of hungry seeking people. At the fifteenth year of our church life, we were holding a congregational meeting to strategize about church growth and ways to make the ministry matter at this time in our development. We spent hours in the pontifical exchange of the learned, the seminary trained, the seasoned leadership with our charts and graphs. And there was absolutely no air of inspiration stirring anywhere in the room.

None.

Then one old mother rose from her chair, recently converted and not yet duly impressed with us, to censor herself. She unceremoniously asked. "Excuse me, Sister Pastor, I hear all this here stuff. But what about *the love?*"

I stood there indicted. Caught in the very act of not being in love with my neighbor. She was right. I was embarrassed by the truth. I was embarrassed by those who heard her, and wanted to pretend they had not. I was embarrassed for my colleagues. I shrank in my own estimation. As a woman new in Christ, but old in age, she shone a light and found a *love-vacancy sign* glaring a neon reality. We had become a cadre of slick church professionals, well educated and well spoken. We were unconsciously competing with the magazine variety wanna-be-a-mega-church strivers.

> *"Without love I become a noisy gong*
> *and a clanging cymbal ..."*

And I dared to judge the Elder Josephs of my past? Truer still, at that moment I realized that neither "institutions" nor formulas, denominations nor local churches, pitiful preachers nor professional pastors, can create love. Nor can they ultimately stop it.

Love always finds a way in, intrusively, persistently because it comes from God, who is faithful when we are not. God has pity on the deadness of our frail efforts. God's Spirit sneaks in on us and comes again and again to warm the heart and offer water to the parched bones. *Individuals in the holy institutions are merely responsible for fostering an environment where love is welcome to stay and grow.*

Yes, Mother Hunter, what about the love?

> *"Ye who do earnestly repent of your sins, and*
> *Who intend to lead a new life,*
> *In love and harmony with your neighbor...*
> *Draw nigh with a full assurance of faith."*

Draw nigh.

Come close.

Listen intently with the faith that it can still happen.

The Capacity for Love

Christians have entrusted love "to a capacity that comes from the Spirit." Indeed the love of God is "shed abroad in our hearts by the Holy Ghost." It is a sure sign of conversion and regeneration from the old death. "By this, shall all men know that you are my disciples, that you love one another." But sometimes, spiritual assurances make us humanly lazy. Knowing this, we have excused ourselves from the part that is our own human responsibility. Women have a responsibility to be well loved in private spaces and not confuse that with what is owed to us from the public spaces. We have a responsibility to be clear, and not indict the "church family," because of those who did not satisfy us from our first family. And we must examine the capacity inside our own hearts *for love to grow, indeed to outgrow the clutter and leftover pain.*

With all our doctrinal correctness, scripture memorization, our choreographed praise, with all our grand structures, trinkets and technology, we stand under indictment. Formally accused. Where is the love that clearly validates Christian transformation? Preachers are blinded by our ego-satisfying ambition, polished advertisements, neighborhood or national campaigns. Inside the well-packaged personae, we seem to eventually leave off the commensurate attention — equal time to loving people. We become jaded. We collect offenses. We are bruised once too often by the abandonment of parishioners we invest in. We see too much of the underside of the human condition. In being professional Christians, the matters of inner space get eclipsed. Our capacity for loving becomes littered by so much debris, and the inner space becomes dark, dank, and over-crowded. Air in the heart becomes still. Un-living.

There are unexamined reasons that love is not on the menu in most Christian conversations.

Love is not for the stupid or the dull. Salvation enlivens!! But *religion* makes us dull. Religion keeps the rules, obeys the script; soon we become dense about that which is truly spiritual. Stupid, in some sense, for in our fear of doing "it" wrongly, we do nothing at all.

It takes a certain *aptitude* to be in love with my neighbor. It demands an ability to pay attention. It presumes a willingness to live in self-forgetful ways, at least enough to give a holy curiosity about the well-being of another. And it demands the skillful tension, wherein curiosity and care never evolve into the posture of control and command.

Love is not for the lazy. It is birthed in the heart by the miracle of grace. It is only *sustained* in the heart by the disciplined attention of daily tending, forgiving, noticing, studying, ignoring what needs to be ignored, and feeding what hungers for your care. Without resentment. Without keeping score.

Love is not for the overly self-conscious. It, by demand, makes one freer than we are comfortable being. Love, in different ways than hatred, loosens the tongue. It opens the hand. It gives us permission to say the warm, lifting, building things we are otherwise too embarrassed to say. Yes, love even *tutors* the mute in finding words that were never gifted to us. Words we heard only in our imagination.

Love is not for the self-absorbed. And most modern professional churchmen and churchwomen live with a fair degree of self-absorption. Whether on pew or parking lot or platform, we are concerned with our own ratings. We are fretful over our own needs or lacks or wants. The self-absorbed will violate the *emotional* boundaries of persons who trust us, just to feel valuable. They engage in "emotional fondling," and when called on it, will protest their ignorance and their innocence. ("You know I didn't mean anything by that...") And they will violate the *physical* boundaries of little girls or boys in holy spaces. They will barter sexual play, too needy to ever consider the impact of what they do; how it damages the soul for good.

This is not love.

The self-absorbed are always the stars of our own shows. We "thing-i-fy" the parishioners, the altar boys, any vulnerable, needy people; the church staff, the adjutants and assistants, all become supporting cast ... to be utilized, to be paid, but seldom to be *seen* as persons, worthy of our respect and our love. We are Christians of the lower case. Small c. But we are seldom lovers.

Finally, love is not for those who are unwilling to suffer. Count up your own needs for love. List the ways in which you need love to satisfy you. Define who you need to love you, and whom you wish to love fully and completely. Then, in order to be love's student, you must be willing to cast it all upon the fires of love's holocaust. *Love, when done God's way, will consume all your well-thought-out boundaries of protection, and silence all your protests and demands.* Love, to be sure, will make you suffer. Willingly. Knowingly. From a position of strength and choice. This is the story of the Cross.

In Love With My Neighbor

That old Mother intuitively inquired that day about the love that had left us in the house of God. We never meant it to happen. If we were liars, we would have protested and denied it. It happens slowly. It happens unintentionally. It happens with the best of motives among the Christians.

But then again who, any more, teaches love? When was the last time any of us heard a lesson, or read a "Christian book" on love and loving? Or heard a sermon on love: its power, its hope, the "how and why"? Love is assumed. It is expected. It is yearned for. It is fraudulently masqueraded, trapping the young in poor fleeting substitutes, and the naïve in "church" advertisement. But at what address is love found? Which school do we enroll in; whose house do we go to, to learn love's language, her behavior, its scent? Is it any wonder that we halt, we stumble and we do without it, instead settling for the paltry substitutes: dreary companionship, mechanical worship, obligatory family connections and empty communion?

In our attention to things and programs, we in the church had *left each other*. Love, given no atmosphere in which to live, gathered her pretty belongings and she left. In her leaving, the corridors of our own ministry became dry, dusty, almost meaningless. It is the love I vow never again to live without.

"Love in the House of God where I am honestly, earnestly in love with my neighbor!" What a thought! The promise of it keeps us coming, week after week, negotiating the crowds, tolerating the irrelevance, drawing near with faith that we will find it, and have a place to give it.

"Draw near

In full assurance of faith..."

Love. Its promise gives us the grace to hear the wonder and see the beauty of our own story, finally seen through merciful eyes: other Christians who have survived, and who now love enough to share the truth of their own redemption. Christian love is our own story, refurbished by the Blood of Christ. We draw near through all the clutter, straining to hear the announcement articulated over and over again each Sunday morning. "I Am the One who has chosen to love you, for no other reason, except for what you may become."

The church has given me so much. She gave me a place to hone my gifts as a child. She insisted on structure for my life when the streets would have claimed me. She held out rules to gird me, in seasons of my own rebellion. She revealed my purpose, a new social reality, and a place to belong. A place to go when I was not invited anywhere else in particular. Filler for my loneliness. An altar for my tears. The church has given me so much. The holy bosom in which I heard the voice of Jesus call me.

I wonder what I have *really* given back in return.

"Yes, Mother Hunter. What about the love?"

Sacramental Theology
Speaks of a
Doctrine of the Real Presence.
Maybe there should be a doctrine of the
Real Absence,
Because absence can be
sacramental too.
A door left open, a chamber of the heart
kept ready and
Waiting.

Frederick Buechner

Chapter Seven
Daddy's Girl

"And why do we fall in love, when we know that eventually it will break our hearts, and leave us inconsolable; when it will only teach us that eventually, we must learn to live without almost every person we love?" the young girl asked. The wise old woman, taking her face into her hands, tenderly replied, "Because loving is what we do best."

Finally it dawns on me.

For most of my life, I have been resisting. I have been guarding my heart, dancing too fast to let *it* encounter me. One can go about rescuing the world in public, and losing one's own soul in very private ways.

I am a preacher woman. I can handle you, help you, hear you. I can fix you, make you feel better and send you on your way: counseled, corrected and comforted. I can leap tall buildings with a single bound, and stop speeding bullets with one hand. It is just that business about connected, meaningful relationship that keeps eluding me.

"Just don't come close. I might want you to stay."

For much of my conscious life in ministry, I have been taught that pure *inspiration* is born in *isolation*. Uncontaminated. The vacuum invites "the more" of God. Therefore, most of my *conscious* life, I have been standing as a sentry, barring the door of my own heart. I have tried to believe that love is "first spiritual," then natural. Really though, only in the scary contexts of natural human, imperfect relationships are genuine love and deep spirituality fermented. Ministers and church professionals are often the most fearful persons when it comes to *people*, even though *people* are our business. We hide safely, camouflaging "skeletons" that parade as the fully formed, skilled people we are supposed to be. We are beautiful in extravagant, bejeweled holy garments. We seem competent with our scriptural formulas. Just don't make us come out from beneath the *role* of "minister." We are great performers, but often poor husbands, insensitive wives, and elusive parents. We secretly fear the success of the colleagues in our neighborhood, because we feel if "they are better ... bigger ..." then "I must be lesser." While we spend our years orchestrating programs and plans for other people's fellowship, ministers avoid fellowship *with each other* on any long-term basis. It would demand taking off the "holy robes." It would demand laying aside our self-imposed busy-ness. We are far more comfortable with our assignments than with our relationships. And too often, we are very successful, very isolated individuals, who look up often, but who seldom look *within*.

Where Does It All Begin?

The "first family," the family we originated from, will always give us scripts. The firstborn may become the "family hero," rescuer, or caretaker of the group. The middle child may become "mediator and peace maker." The baby of the family may be tagged the "spoiled child," expecting to be catered to and cared for. And on it goes. And usually persons who are "called to ministry" hear that call *within the context of some* echo from the "first family." The roles that we eventually assume in ministry are very telling.

The *pastor* may have been the "family hero." This child may have been well nurtured among a web of relationships, or may be the person who was left outside the relationships he or she longed for. Nevertheless, he or she now spends adult life trying to make it happen for others: care-taking and orchestrating. The *traveling evangelist* may have been the child who had rather loosely formed connections from the beginning: it is easy *to go into all the world*, all the time, because there was never much at home worth staying for. The fiery *prophet* was probably validated as a child by bossing, correcting and telling on her other siblings; feeling the inward pull to straighten out the "dysfunction" of her little world. Or the prophet may have been the most injured child, now bent to demand justice, or to defend the oppressed and misused. The *mystic* may have been an only child, who learned early to commune, think and figure out the world, its secrets, and its mysteries, alone. "First families" prepare us for our second ones — the second natural family of adult life and the *spiritual* family.

In God's providence, our "first families" bend us toward our search for God.

When any loved man leaves, you try to adjust, land on your feet and at least appear to recover. This is because when the First Man in your life left you, something prepared you then. You absolutely refuse to be left again ... not in that way. So you sort of close up shop. You put a "no vacancy" sign on the door to ward off the curious, and you do emotional business through a half-open window. Even long after you are called to preach.

*

"The little girl sat at the kitchen table as the sun went down. She absorbed herself in the assignment, though she secretly knew she did not have to try hard to please her teachers. She knew from her history she would do well. That is how she got noticed. That is how she bartered for smiles, nods of attention, for love. That is how she swam to the top, through the muddy mass of little colored children, to get the love she wanted from the nice white teachers. Do well. Be nice. Perform.

She had just come back to the kitchen table after pulling herself away from the free time she allowed herself after school. She spent most of her time alone in her room. Often she played a game where she became someone else. You should have seen her, with a half-slip on her head, hanging down her back as she magically gave herself the same long, flowing yellow hair of the Irish or German pretty-white-girl school friends she secretly admired. She snuck dabs of her mama's rouge and lipstick, and painted her face; she stole a cigarette from her daddy's drawer and let it hang from her lips and bob up and down as she talked to a pretend friend. She put on her mama's high heel shoes over her knee socks, and sang along to the mirror with a bottle of White Shoulders perfume or a hairbrush as her microphone. Dinah Washington, Dakota Staton or Billie Holiday on record albums, or even Arthur Prysock could be her pretend voice. It did not matter.

She pretended the audience adored her and for those few hours, they really did.

She had been "primping" in the mirror, as her Daddy called it; she had to hurry and get to her assignment. "Primping." If she had a word for it, it would be nothing so frivolous. To her 12-year-old soul, it was "seeking" or "searching" or auditioning for life. The inquiry of a 12-year-old; she was looking for mirrors in her atmosphere to assure her she was worthwhile.

Being abandoned by childhood, and pushed into a new category of femaleness that is yet unfamiliar, little girls need mirrors to explain things. Is the changing body, her hair, her newfound ticklish curiosity really a safe place to live? They need to know how to feel grounded as they tumble, arms and legs all akimbo, and hope they will land into adulthood on their feet. And when they land, what roles they will be allowed to play, and with whom? And who will be there with her? Who can she count on to stay? The one mirror that never betrayed the little girl was her Daddy's face. There in his eyes she was Beautiful. Safe. Loved. Daddy's girl.

Abruptly, she was startled from her kitchen table reverie. The door from upstairs that opened onto the kitchen, swung open. There was her Daddy. As always, he was beautiful to her eyes. Brown skin; proud forehead; the Indian hook of his nose; the way he smelled; the way he smiled. Her heart always stood on tiptoes when he entered her space. He was her hero. Her larger than life Father. What God must be like, though she did not know for sure if there was a God. But she knew for sure there was her Daddy. Even when he was displeased with her (though she never ever wanted him to be!), or challenging her about some behavior, some grade, some way of sitting or holding her fork, he was her refuge. She warmed at his constant fires.

Strange. At eight o'clock in the evening, the Daddy had a pile of suits slung over his arms, and was making his way out the kitchen door to the car. She froze; she kept doing her homework, refusing to look up. He kept marching up and down the stairs, in the ritual of divestiture, refusing to look down at her eye to eye. Finally, the Mama came down and the little girl could hear muffled tones in the hallway. The little girl strained to hear. But she was stuck to her seat at the kitchen table, and dared not get up. Could anybody hear inside her head as she wrote her history lesson with a hand disconnected from her mind? She was screaming, shrieking, crying out loud inside her thoughts. But there she sat.

"Where are you going ... my Daddy!! Oh no, please don't leave me ... Daddy, please don't leave me!!!"

But she wrote in her best penmanship, tomorrow's lesson. Daddy always said, *If it is worth doing, it's worth doing well.* Mr. Patterson, the seventh grade teacher, would never, ever catch her unprepared. And Daddy always said *to finish what you start.*

Waves of vomit fought to come to her mouth. *And she kept writing.*

Terror, as heavy and steely as any grown woman would ever carry, climbed up into the little girls bowels. *And she kept writing.*

When any loved man leaves, you try to adjust, land on your feet and at least appear to recover. This is because when the First

Man in your life leaves you, something has prepared you already. You absolutely refuse to be left again ... not in that way. So you sort of close up shop. You put a "no vacancy" sign on the door to ward off the curious, and you do emotional business through a half open window. Indeed, the vacancy is the thing you carry around in your soul, each minute. Even long after you are called to preach.

"You can reach me at Lee Daniels' house if you all need anything ... if you change your mind." The mother said something, and the door closed.

And the Daddy was gone.

She wanted to run down the street shrieking, begging, pleading with her daddy to please stay. She would not primp so much in the mirror, and she would always clean up the kitchen just right, and ... whatever, *whatever* it took, she would be a good girl and never, ever get in trouble at school, or be a bother. Instead, she sat there at the kitchen table, vinyl chairs stuck to her hot feverish brown legs. *And she kept writing. She stayed glued to her assignment. Eyes fastened to her paper. She had an assignment due in the morning. Her daddy would want her to do well.*

Fathers and Futures

What we enjoy of good fathering is the way the taste of it lingers in the mouth, long after the substance has been swallowed up, digested and lived off. The way one finds a surprise morsel stuck in a back tooth that still holds the flavor of a meal long gone. Who could know that you never *did* get quite enough when you sat to enjoy it? So you take the taste into your future.

I am replaying the childhood comforts of sitting on Daddy's lap, my ear to his chest. I am counting his heartbeats and contemplating the mystery of the hairs on his chin and in his nostrils as he watched "Gunsmoke" on the black and white television and smoked Pall Mall cigarettes. There, I learned my first notions of what man-love was supposed *to feel* like, smell like, act like. That love was an ever-widening possibility. It was so very real, though so very "other," very opposite from my own little girl world. A grateful memory. Today, a morsel still. I stood adoringly, watching my Daddy at the mirror, following him into the yard, watching him at the stove cooking two eggs over easy, with toast and apple butter. He never shooed me away, like a bothersome puppy or a crowding presence, the way I have seen parents do. Does a daughter first learn the wonder of worship, gazing at the father-man who was larger than life to her? It was he who admonished me about the correct way to brush my teeth and to be proud of my high forehead, for, he lectured my six-year-old ears, *all truly intelligent* women had them (pointing out pictures of Mamie Eisenhower and the Duchess of Windsor as newspaper proof). *Daddy said*, never hide my huge forehead under my bangs, and so it was. Like so many other things he gave me, my father's nearness and his words gave me definition for my future as a woman.

Fathers and Foundations

I learned the matrix of love here. I learned to adore a certain kind of man, as I watched *him, the First Man*, reading books, books, books; and dressing for his evening's work at the "after hours gambling joint" he owned. I learned to *expect* to be called "baby" and "sugar" by a man; I came to savor the beautiful man-smell of him in his tailored suits and starched, French-cuffed white shirts, gold cuff links and gentle kisses on my lips assuring me of his love and his soon-return in the morning. "When you wake up, Daddy will be home." And he always was. Awakening me for school, chiding me for being a lazybones, or threatening to throw ice water under my sheets.

Father-foundation is a grateful memory. Even thirty years after laying him down in the grave, I wish still for his presence at my table. I am ambushed by a longing for his counsel and his lap, as life leaves me with an ever-narrowing group of male comforters. So few teachers now. So few guides.

How could he leave his little girl that day, who needed him so, and never come back again?

Today, who provides for us safe male places to be naked and needing? Who models, who teaches us the value of creating good memories for each other — early in the relationship — which we will so desperately need later, when loving gets dim? Who makes the arrangements for learning to trust the men in our tomorrows? Who bequeaths our sons and daughters with a sense of value, protection, worth, and identity? Father-foundations say to you and to *your world* that you are important. "Look! Behold! See? *This* is my beloved, and in her, I am well-pleased."

No matter. As women of a certain breed, we wait, we work, we go on. We sit erect at the table of our assignments. We look straight ahead in church pews, under pretty hats; or on the judge's bench under stern black robes; or behind desks, or factory walls, or bedroom doors. We do well. We finish what we start. We make our own money. We get promoted. We break glass ceilings and we raise our children to excel. We say it loud: *I am here. I am competent. I am unafraid. And it does not matter that I, and now my children, are alone.*

When a loved man leaves, you try to adjust, land on your feet and at least appear to recover. This is because the First Man in your life has left you, and you are prepared. You absolutely refuse to be left again ... not in that way. So you sort of close up shop. You put a "no vacancy' sign on the door to ward off the curious, and you do emotional business through a half open window.

And finally, you learn to do business with God.

"First families" prepare us for our second ones. Naturally and spiritually. Empty spaces create eternal opportunities for The Father. Sometimes, the most profound caverns house the most tremendous opportunities for the *assignment.* Early on, the little girl learns to look past the vacancies, work in spite of who abandons her and stick to the assignments she is given.

And for her comfort and her consolation, there is the precious Anointing.

The most incredible hungers ignite the most ravenous seeking.

And finding.

Handed off from one daddy, to Another.

Daddy's girl. Always.

Whither is thy beloved gone

O thou fairest among women?

Whither is thy beloved turned aside?

That we may

seek

him

with

thee.

Song of Solomon, Chapter Six

Chapter Eight
What's Love Got To Do With It?

Such was the question of pop music diva Tina Turner, who gave voice to a generation of skeptical, love-weary disenchanted Americans. "...Nothing but a second hand emotion." What's love got to do with it, Ms. Tina? With all our pretended disengagement, with all our independence and looking-straight-ahead *nonchalance*, love is still the only thing we continue to hope for, wish for, grieve over, pretend we don't need, run from or run for, till we die.

The Grateful Memory

It is the manner in which one's present life is arranged, vis-à-vis one's past.

My earliest memory of love is a game my mother played with me. At bedtime kisses, we would say, "I love you more than all the..." and each night try to out-imagine the other in the wideness of our affection. "More than all the snowflakes that ever fell." "More than all the drops of water in the ocean." "More than all the grains of sand on all the beaches in the world." And on it went. These were my first inklings of what love was supposed to *sound like*. Gentle. Unafraid. Accepting. And it still sounds the same today, in moments of unguarded admission, about the ways a mother always loves her daughter, and the ways a daughter always craves her mother's love.

Love is a grateful memory. A smell of clean, crisp sheets at the end of a hard day of playing outside. A welcoming aroma of turnip and mustard greens boiling, or pork chops frying or blueberry cobbler baking, 'cause it meant Mama didn't have to go to work that day, and was mine-all-mine, if just for now. Love is the grateful memory, which bequeathed me the security to tip into adulthood as though I was really ready for it.

A lifetime later, watching the mother once so strong and all-knowing, now with changing looks and stories she forgot that she has already told me, I recall her strength and her lessons and her cornbread. My heart is swept with a nostalgia that forgives all the debts that daughters hold, and forgets all the ways I thought it should have been different. I know it as love. Gift love. Need love.

It is a life-sustaining memory, this recollection.

The Arrangements of Love

Love is presumed between mother and child — that instinctual thing that is said to rise from the very soul of a woman when she sets eyes on that moist, squirming, helpless thing, escaped from her womb for the first time.

Love is the feeling of dependency that a child has for his mother or father when the child has been consistently satisfied. C.S. Lewis calls it, *need love* and *gift love.* "I need you, so I love you." Love is that "sense" which I have learned to trust, for its constancy, for its pure generosity and unconditional survival benefit.

Concurrently then, the sense in which *I meet* your needs, defines my "worth and value" in your eyes. It feels like love to us both. I alone am able to express the proverbial "breast milk," the sustenance for one who needs me, in ways that (I need to believe) no other person can satisfy.

Everyone wants to believe in the myth of exclusivity. Divorced persons marry again to feel like they are the "one and only" to someone, even if it proved false in the last marriage. Mamas are jealous for their children's love, and secretly stung the first time their child prefers the home, the attention or the counsel of some other adult, above your own. Daddies want to be the heroes of their child's imagination. The only. The greatest. The strongest in the whole wide world. The one who can fix anything, and right any wrong. When I have emotional ownership, the position, the preeminence in the life of another who *needs me*, I come to *need their need*. I come to label the thing between us as "love." Love is an idea that comes along with certain arrangements. If we are together like this, long enough, then the thing between us must be love.

The Danger of Love

For certain, love is dangerous. Why else would so few risk it?

Love is the willing exposure to the robbers on the road winding downward from Jerusalem to Jericho. Love is the rescue by me, the stranger, when I really have something more pressing and far less inconvenient to do. Love is the gift to one who can never, ever repay me in kind. One whom God defines as my neighbor. The risk is my own vulnerability. The same things that attack your life just might get to mine. Love is dangerous, because it will always cost me to love. I will have to tear my own clothes to cover and aid you, because when I love truly, I discern your nakedness. Even before you mean to show me. It is my response as I bandage your AIDS-tainted blood with my bare hands. By associating with your pain, I risk leaving myself uncovered. I will have to see it. I will have to "get involved." I will have to feel something. I will have to be affected. Love is the danger of making my own life messy, of being late for my planned life. Love is dangerous, for I can never count on exactly when its opportunities or its challenges will appear.

Love is superimposed as a name on the chemistry between lovers — a look, a connection, the "one soul in two bodies" knowing. I was told of a brain chemical that lasts about nine months and is entirely depleted by four years into the relationship of persons "in love." But for any person who has known "falling in love," such mystery could never be reducible to chemicals or body fluids. We insist!! It is *love*. And it is, with all its breath-stopping, consequence-suspending wonder — nothing less than absolute, wonderful *danger*. It is sure to hurt me, mutilate my heart and alter me more than any other thing I will ever know. And I shall be willing, once I have caught its scent.

Love, on one hand, suspends the conscience. For it, we will betray our parents, defy our teachers and our preachers, and ignore race, class or creed. Some will even abandon their children and abdicate positions of power for its allure. Even the saved, the holy, the righteous, when well-enough smitten, have been known to forsake our historical covenants and vows, leaving a trail of broken victims behind us, solely for

the imagined promise of love's delights. No guarantees needed. For being in love feels, for the moment, enough compensation for whatever I must leave behind. Love pays me back
for it all. Love suspends the conscience. And what could be
more dangerous?

On the other hand, as it relates to *the beloved*, it holds the
lover's conscience *captive*. Conscience becomes the willing
servant to the tyranny of love, so that we allow no hint, no
thought of discontent in the beloved. Conscience is formed by
love. Conscience operates because love steers it. The
sociopath, the serial killer, the career criminal in some
respect, never had (or never made) the connection between
knowing he was well-loved; loving well in return; and devel-
oping the *outgrowth of conscience* that inevitably occurs in the
transaction.

> "Love will not eat,
>
> Aware that the beloved hungers,
>
> Nor drink, lest the cup be shared
>
> Down to the last sweet dregs."

With all its danger and illusions, with all that is foolish and
irrational, this too is love.

The season of being in love is a magical, hypnotic state coloring the entire world when the beloved is in it. It makes my
enemies shrink. Their conspiracies are not so threatening.
Gives my soul a refuge, in the midst of every battle, to which
I can retreat. It is the place I can go, if only in my own mind,
and know that *you are on my side.*

> "When in disgrace with fortune and men's eyes
>
> I all alone be-weep my outcast state

And trouble deaf heaven with my bootless cries

And look upon myself and curse my fate...

...Yet in these thoughts myself almost despising,

Haply I think on thee — then my state

Like the lark at break of day arising

From sullen earth, sings hymns at heaven's gate.

For thy sweet love remembered, such wealth brings

That I scorn to change my state with kings."

(Sonnets XXIX, Shakespeare)

So what if, by its very nature, it cannot last in this same way? Love is fickle.

So what, if it allures me, beacons me, then disappears when I try to get my hands around it? So what, if love becomes something altogether different in texture and form, once she comes to stay. Love is illusory. So what that it has demanded all? Stripped away my pretense and my hiding; lain me bare and undefended before her. Silly. Foolish. Willing. So what, if — despite all its promises and lavish assurances — it lasts only for a little while?

Some would say the lessons learned from danger are the ones we never forget. And in some sense, for the beloved you would do it all over again. Love, with all its dangers, teaches us the walk and the reward of faith.

Believing all things.

Hoping all things for the beloved

Never keeping a record of wrong.

Yielding.

Seeing only the best. Jumping in with no guarantee.

Believing, if only for a short space, that love will never let you fall. Is it any wonder that the writer asserts, God *is* love?

The Accidents of Love

We do not choose whom we will fall in love with. Not really. The accidents of chemistry, time, shared context and similar troubles often throw persons together, and unearth love that was not bidden. We do not choose whom we will fall in love with.

We may choose which loves we will hold to, cultivate, work with, commit to. But not whom we will fall in love with.

Some say they have only loved once and truly in a lifetime. Rare souls, I think. I suggest we may fall in love many times in our lives. Whether briefly or fully. Whether hastily buried or fully excavated. Whether accidentally, or as a reward to prayer. Whether admitted or denied. Celebrated or censored. Accidentally, unbidden, if we are fully conscious, we may fall in love many times.

There will be the love of youth. So naïve at seventeen, weren't we, with all the time in the world to dream of how "'life is going to be." Then we had all the strength and vigor to believe we could make it so. So much leeway to make mistakes. So much resilience to recover. So open to learn, to fumble, to nervously discover who we are in the eyes of that first adoring "other." This young love is so militant, with all its blinders — strutting, blustering, daring the world to prove it wrong. We smile at it now, when we spy out this love in the young, and we remember with a knowing that only the years can bring — that they will be disappointed for sure, and puzzled by its changes. But we smile, and for them we hope for the exceptions. They did not choose it. They were chosen by it. God has kissed them.

And who can say it is not truly love, though it is so totally different from the thing we feel at thirty-three or at forty-seven? The love of mid-life has a different task: to see beyond the frayed edges, the gently used pages of a life already well in progress. This love, though you seem to have stumbled upon it once you stopped searching for it, smiles in wonder and finds celebration for what can still be. This love now makes *decisions* to be with you *and* your children and your physical problems; him *and* his child support payments and bills; his "exes" and all. You find the delight of being together not one bit diminished. Love at this stage finds added strength for the added baggage.

The loves of life are often ironic and cruel. They happen. They grow in soil where other crops have already been planted. They peek up through the cracks of what was supposed to be concrete. They do not belong *here*, these loves. They are accidents.

So love becomes the victim of propriety. Stuffed back into convention. What is right. Trained to obey the rules of our society, our church, our family. Love is censored because of our already married state. Our spiritual commitments. Love is stained by the shame of conscience and the shaming of significant others when we are pulled to color outside the lines, and taste what is forbidden. Love becomes deformed when it stays too long in an arrangement that cannot water it, tend it, handle it with some measure of oxygenating care. Though its very nature is to fight for its own existence — defiant, insistent, love finally realizes that it must have an atmosphere of sunshine, not darkness, in order to survive. Love must be celebrated, or she will eventually wither. When housed in darkrooms of secrecy, shame, sneaking and subterfuge, love changes into something small. Love, even in its own accidental nature, still recognizes right from wrong.

Even though it was accidental, it tries to stay; love would like to live a long life right here. Love wants to defer its hour. It hangs on, bearing all things, hoping all things.

But because of Who love really is, love in many ways is willing to become a victim. *True love* lays down its own life, before anyone can take it. Slain. Sacrificed, so that something we call *greater* might live. Some human love, like a grain of wheat, is allowed to fall to the ground and die.

Then there is the hope. That once it is resurrected again, in different form, it will be better; it will be healthier for the many, the all. The children. The ministry. The souls attached to your witness. The God of your life. Loving God anew, afresh, becomes the greatest investment of your whole life. It alone brings accidental loves to the altar of fire, surrenders them, and gives you power to stand upright again. *God's love alone instructs* me what love, indeed, has to do with everything.

The Reparation of Love

Love can fix people. Love is the way God places God's self inside another person called a friend, and presents God's self to you. Love is that wondrous, strengthening bond that neither of us *had* to make because of blood or clan. It is greatest because it is voluntary. Friendship is the love that repairs. The romanticized, idealized attraction of friend for friend makes the days richer and more alive when shared with each other — secrets and confidences and dreams and encouragements. Friend — in whose eyes you look and find truth and approval, even in failure, and despite family verdicts long ago pronounced. It is not about Eros, not the fire, the passionate magnetism that yearns for genital contact or physical expression. No, it is about simply the person in totality. The gift he or she brings to your life, and by that presence, repairs the holes.

And Jonathan and David made a covenant
Because he loved him as his own soul.
(1 Samuel 18:3)

And at the death of Jonathan, David lamented, and cried unashamedly for his friend.

I am distressed for thee, my brother Jonathan
Very pleasant thou hast been unto me.
Thy love to me was wonderful
Passing the love of women.
(2 Samuel 1:26)

Ruth and Naomi. Hepburn and Tracy. Thelma and Louise. Oprah and Gail. Celie and Ms. Shug Avery. With its distortions and inherent imperfections, love repairs. The love of one true friend provides us the "corrective emotional experience" that can heal adult life.

Love fixes people. Who among us cannot point to places

and times of neglect in our families that left us emotionally bereaved? God sends the love of friends as compensation for families who functioned too inadequately to love us generously and specifically.

The accidental loves are not always about lovers.

They are sometimes about the loving friendships that save our lives.

The Fear of Love

What is there about love that makes us so-called evangelical, spirit-filled Christians — strange and uncomfortable? We give. We hug. We eat. We fellowship. When called upon to love, as a rule we stop short.

What happens to love once people become firmly ensconced in our brand of Christianity? Passion is feared. The laughter and easiness of loving and being loved fades. In Christian marriages, the welcoming exchange of daily tenderness and bodily fluids and comforts, having and holding our own mates, from all appearances is forgotten. And in favor of ... what? The very basic people skills of forming and maintaining relationships are scarce in the sanctuary.

This is the problem.

Love makes us *suspicious.* There is an unconscious, uneasy suspicion about love and loving. It would seem that love could only make for a collective improvement in all of life. How could it make us worse on any front? Yet when love enters the domain of human church folks — of a certain brand — a kind of uneasiness comes, too. The ones who are touched by it, and the ones who seem to be outside its circle of warmth, are brushed by love's suspicions. Why? Because, love by its very nature, *excludes*. It elevates *one* to an exclusive position. By doing so, it leaves the other in the realm of the ordinary. What should be a cause for celebration, "that he loves her," by implication points to the places where "he nor anyone loves me" — at least like that. They love *each other*, as a group of friends. But somehow if that circle does not reach around *to me,* then *their* love feels suspicious, cold and exclusive as a "clique." If they go to that church, or that denomination, they have not just been blessed by a new possibility for growth. They have *left us.* They have left *me.* It is a love that saddens me, clouding its own beauty because I cannot partake for myself. Love feels suspicious.

Secondly, love calls up our *expectations.* In the context of love, for the first time I allow myself all the regressive, unreasonable, wished-for, infantile fantasies about how important I wish to be to another human being. In adult love, I try to re-master and re-construct all the places where I was not loved adequately as a child. So once I have become comfortable, really, *really* comfortable and safe, my lover begins to pay for all the unmet expectations I ever had in love. I strut. I grasp. I demand. Love is juxtaposed over against expectations. A contest in the subconscious. And soon *expectations* outweigh love as *the indicator* for the life of our relationships. Please me. Satisfy me. Perform for me. Then I will know you love me.

Thirdly, besides *suspicion* and *expectation,* human love is fearful and so troublesome because of its daring, *freeing* quality. Most religion is designed to control outcomes. Love frees for the possibilities. Religion constructs knowable parameters, fences, walls between this and that, us and them. To be sure, were it not for the constraints of our religion, or any religion, society would implode upon itself in a heap of disorder, chaos and probably destruction. Religion underpins laws. Religion infuses even the humanist's world with a higher code of right and wrong boundaries.

But love also loosens individuals *from* the constraints. That is why, on some level, Christians are so afraid of love. We need rules. We will take or leave the love. Love takes into account the rules, and then transcends them.

"Desire spiritual gifts ... but ... I show unto you a more excellent way."

"Woman, you were caught in the very act of adultery ... But neither do I condemn you. Go, and sin no more."

"Zaccheus, thief, extortionist, today I must come to your house."

"This man receives sinners, and eats with them."

"Go tell my disciples, and Peter, who feels he is disqualified, to meet me..."

We fear love.

It permeates walls and boundaries and keep-out signs.

Love grins, then knowingly leaps anyway.

Weightless.

Conscious of the cost of washing your feet in full view of the crowd, and having a hunch that you have the capacity to betray me, I get out the basin and the towel, and grasp you by ankle.

Love feels very, very dangerous. No wonder we make little room for it.

Love. We readily admit our need for it. We handily espouse the theological underpinnings of "walking in love" as the summary of our Decalogue. But it is more manageable, more comfortable, living out of our heads, out of our scripts, out of our mutual exchanges. We can readily learn the rules. But living from love ... *that* is another thing. Something that makes us feel so good, and act so freely and behave so selflessly, must be dangerous.

What's love got to do with it, Ms. Tina?

It is the only thing that

Never, ever

Fails.

Somebody call my mama, and tell her
I said, "Pray for me."
Somebody call my mama, and tell her
please pray for me.
Tell her that her boy is in trouble
Down here broken-hearted as he can be.

Traditional Blues Tune

Chapter Nine
I Never Said I'm Sorry

Betrayal is never an easy subject.

To speak of the ways in which one *has been betrayed* is to expose one's own inferiority, one's own poverty of value. It is to advertise one's powerlessness to hold the love and loyalty of one's beloved. To be betrayed is to abdicate the illusion of exclusivity. It is to admit that, at least *in that* instance, I did not matter in the ways that I trusted and presumed. Betrayal is the terrorizing admission that the emotional structures that have supported your world in some orderly sense have now collapsed into a heap of falsehood. It is to fall headlong. Betrayal is the sense of freefalling, willing to grasp anything or anyone that will staunch the feeling of worthlessness. It is to become horribly paranoid, fearful, shaken at the prospect of living in connection with friend or lover, ever again.

To own the ways in *which one has betrayed others* is even a more awkward and shame-filled discussion. It is to confess sin. It is to have one's face rubbed in the deficiency in one's own character. To admit betraying another admits enthroning your own desires and comforts above the faithful demand of God. It is my calling to preach faithfulness. It is my conviction that faithfulness is among the greatest of holy virtues. Yet, despite what I know and believe, I can recall profoundly significant events in my life in which I have been faithless. I have acted as the betrayer.

I have in small ways betrayed a friend, by not defending her. I have entered carelessly into a conversation that exposed a confidence. I have omitted a word or an action that allowed me to have the pre-eminence, at the expense of one I loved. I have withheld my care for a family member, because of my own laziness, judgment or apathy. I have betrayed my husband in some of the awful ways that only married persons can hurt and damage each other.

And I have betrayed the God of my life, who entrusted me with His influence.

I want to believe that the times have been few. Yet they were profoundly significant junctures. I have swapped godly influence *for personal affection.* To speak mercifully about betrayers of God, maybe it occurs most readily when our *pain* outweighs our *shame* at doing so. Anything for now, to make one feel better. At the time, I called it loneliness. In retrospect I call it deception, or weakness. In my most honest moments, I call it "wanting to." There were men whom God entrusted to my influence. I drew them to myself instead.

Preachers / pastors have been deputized to act on God's behalf. I have been commissioned, sent into the world with the mantle of ministry draped upon my life. God arranged contexts, appointments, meetings in which God desired an entrance *through* the preacher's life. And, in some of those times, I betrayed God.

Influence is a tricky thing. It is a heady thing. It is mandatory for effective leadership. It must be harnessed wisely to stand before people weekly in a holy spotlight. It demands strict stewardship as you serve on a staff, work in an institution or ride the assisting second-seat. Just a bit of influence will deceive you about your own ability. Influence is the "baby sister" of power. It is the first, unspoiled half of manipulation. Influence can be the wind beneath the wings, or the storm that destroys. It sits at the door always ready to seduce the un-thoughtful. Influence, when owned by women, is often submerged, camouflaged, even denied, lest it seem too threatening to the partner she loves. This too, is a betrayal of the God who loaned it to her.

I have always had influence. From the days of Mr. Garfunkle's 4th grade classroom when I was chosen as the classroom monitor, to elementary school class presidencies, to girl-gangs in junior high, to the most likely to succeed in high school, influence came easily. Influence does not pair necessarily, with the exceptionally brilliant, the stunningly beautiful or the particularly ambitious or sociable. It is the intangible gift of being able to move and guide the outcomes of other people's lives ... with their voluntary cooperation.

Influence.

Perhaps it is God's grace for ministry, God's preparation for the calling.

And I suspect it is God's greatest test for the integrity of ministry, and the greatest danger of the assignment. People have easily opened their lives, their stories, their secrets to me, unbidden. They gave me unconditional positive regard.

And sometimes, they have even given me their love.

I have not always used it honorably.

*

I watched his back. A big, hulking frame, walking slowly away like a little boy unjustly punished. It was his admirable effort to hold on to the remnants of dignity. He had carefully re-gathered himself. Composed now, but swollen from his unabashed weeping: Please, why are you doing this to me, Claudette? My replies sounded hollow, flimsy, even to me. They had the ring of a convenient excuse, covered over with spiritual props. Reassembled, he turned away. Crushed. Brutalized. In Jesus Name.

I would see him from time to time around the huge college campus. But after two years of sharing the fabric of daily life and nightly study and laughter, food and tears, secrets and dreams, prayers and scripture, that day was the last time we ever spoke.

Mine was the love of the meantime. Mine was the affection of the immature, untutored, still careless in the handling of human hearts. This was the girl, unskilled at the ways that spiritual love is called to honor human relationship. I had not yet learned that influence *is mandated* to honor the boundaries. In the matter of human relationships, spiritual influence *has access* to places that it must never *invade*, in the human hearts. Preachers have an advantage that they are never to take. They are not to take advantage of people's gifts or people's affections, which belong only to God. Mine was the love of "for now." Mine was the love of coloring outside the lines, just this time, just this once. It was that compartmentalized thing that young girls can do, like trying on an expensive outfit that both you and the saleslady know you cannot afford to buy — and keeping it on a bit too long because after all — it looks and feels so good. Then, inexplicably, the garment gets ripped or torn or soiled. Ruined. The horror is deeper than embarrassment. It is the shame of knowing that for this, I simply cannot pay. I should never have presumed to put it on in the first place.

It is that compartmentalized thing that some old preacher men do, telling the weak, the hurting and the trusting that there is permission for them to dabble "affectionately." Their "spiritual" position presumes an emotional privilege. This liberty as a young woman preacher, as a Christian who knew better, was a betrayal of a young man's faith. Most basically, it was the careless handling of the God in my life. This relationship would not be the portrait of my real life in Christ, but nonetheless, I was seeing ... trying on ... how I would look inside this man's landscape.

We were 19 or 20. Young. But we were grown enough for roots to have solidified in the soil of our affections on cold Connecticut evenings. *It does not feel like betrayal at the* time. It felt like the comfort of two outsiders, thrust into the excluding white culture of New England in the 70's. We were two "make-good" children of the ghetto, carrying the hopes and dreams of our families and our race on our backs. *Here we were, ladies and gentlemen,* finding our way onto a college campus, and doing our best to survive the crushing foreignness of it all.

His was the love of the virginal ... innocent, willing, pure. The love ripe from years of outside-ness and imperfect connections. A father who died far too early, and the array of deprivations that happen to boys in poor families, with clingy, over-dependent mothers, and uncaring ghetto arrangements. His love was a gift given blindly and generously, without history to inform him of the dangers.

Oh, I loved him to be sure. That is what makes betrayal even more treacherous and sad. He evoked that thing in a young girl that makes her want to care for a man. That thing that makes her feel competent, powerful and valued because he responds to *her*. The Goddess. He introduced me to Roberta Flack and brought me peanut butter and jelly sandwiches on snowy weekend evenings when the dining room was closed. He trusted me with his vulnerability, his poet's sensitivity. He wrote words I alone had inspired. My body became the highway shrine at which he worshiped.

Some loves have their beginnings in prohibited soil. Some relationships are "plantings" in places immediately hostile to any future. Their lives alone would choke any hope of flowering and proliferation. "Some seed was sown on rock…"

*

Ideologies can hold us in proximity to each other. Values hold us in covenant, in responsible patterns of behavior, till our emotions recover their sensibilities. Ideologies and values keep us in dry marriage seasons, until the love returns. "What we believe" will constrain us to maintain responsible, even sacrificial relationship to children who are often ungrateful, rebellious and who break our hearts. Ideologies bind us to the Christian community, despite irrelevant sermons, hurtful relationships and unbalanced personal tending.

We do the right thing, eventually, because we *believe* the right thing.

Ideologies, vows and Christian ideals are what keep society from imploding and collapsing into a rubble heap. Belief systems keep us from wandering all over the emotional globe, doing whatever feels good at the time. Biblical Christianity provides the skeletal system for the life of the believer.

Line upon line.

Precept upon precept.

Bone connected to bone.

It keeps us formed. Straight. Upright again. In the inner place, the "thing I believe" keeps me true to God.

Or it alerts me, when it is God I am betraying.

My holy, righteous belief system is my plumb line. My true north star. The homing device which insures that I am picked up on God's radar.

It keeps us clear in the matter of relationship.

I am saved. You are not.

> *Be not unequally yoked together with unbelievers.*
>
> *Have no fellowship with the unfruitful works of dark-*
>
> *ness, rather reprove them.*

No one mentions the ways in which ideologies, in imma-ture hands, can be toxic. They become weapons against the human spirit. What we hold as the dearest and most impor-tant beliefs can also be the things that smother, shame and prohibit the purest gifts of love. We are black; they are not. We are white; they are not. We are educated; they are not. We are Irish, Italian, Greek; we are of this class, or that; we are ... and they are not.

I am saved. You are not.

It became a platform for my own superiority.

It became a haunting reality when I was listening to God.

It became my excuse when my affections for the young

man were vacillating.

God had given me influence, to be used for God. I bartered it when I needed the young man's company or his kindness. I wielded it when I needed God's favor.

I, the Lord your God am a jealous God, having no other Gods before me.

"I will exalt myself above the throne of God."

I, the Lord your God am a Jealous God, having no other Gods before me.

"You will not surely die."

I, the Lord your God am...

One day I just sent him away. Abruptly. In ways he could not understand, and I could not explain. I was tired of wrestling with God, but the damage had already been done.

I am saved. You are not.

You are saved, but you are not spiritual enough.

You are spiritual, but you do not have the Holy Ghost.

You are none of / all of these things. But you are probably more righteous than I.

No wonder he could not understand. I had betrayed God, and in doing so, the young man suffered the harshest of all betrayals.

I had co-mingled the *spiritual* with the sensual, in ways that had become indistinguishable. When a woman swaps Godly influence for her own personal affection, there is no seam when you want one or the other back. I had given him Jesus and me. In ways that now felt like a death to him he was asked to settle for the One, without the other.

When a Christian leader, man or woman, *mixes sensual presence* into spiritual relationship, there evolves an illegal permanence, whether intended or not. There arises a binding from this blending, which resists ending. It hints at a kind of marriage, which in order to end, must rip, and tear, and sometimes shred the heart. That is why some affections should only be sampled within the context of holy, permanent vows.

When the Christian mixes *spiritual influence*, disregards boundaries and tampers with the sensual, the influence is always made stronger *at first*. But at last it is tainted. For the Christian, this mixing always points to the inevitability of impermanence. *I will have no other Gods before me.* When you disregard the boundary, you most often lose the relationship. Or something good that was central to it. God will see to it. David's encounter with Bathsheba, Uriah's wife, is so very telling. The baby born of their adulterous love was stricken.

"And David lay all night on the ground, and fasted,
that perhaps God would let the child live."

No David, the child will die.

The child of the flesh has to die, or you will never conceive the child of the Spirit. Dissolution becomes the only resolve; one has to clean it out in order to start all over again. "I want to do it right next time."

God I am so sorry. And so messy. Messy.

No matter how spiritual we deem ourselves, there are ways in which we are stupid about the rituals of parting kindly. In my righteousness, I bludgeoned a heart, and set a life reeling off course. As far as I could tell, he never recovered. To God, I repented. I resumed my life of scripted holiness. Graduated. Went on with my life. But to the young man, I never said, "I am sorry."

*

Twenty-five years later. An eerie, almost tangible presence is in my room. I have only experienced these times of encounter two or three times in my life. I am an admitted skeptic when I talk to the mystics. Some saints traffic in the easily supernatural, and talk of angels and spirits with familiarity. I do not tout soul travel or out of body experiences. I curse the very idea of those who seek communion with the departed. But on that morning, 25 years later ... what was it? Was it a dream, this presence standing on the side of my bed, staring long, long, long. As if waiting patiently for something. As if just coming to see for himself. As if waiting for a response to his presence. And there I lay, penetrated by silent, sad, solitary eyes. Disturbed out of my sleep, I knew ... it was him. Then it was over.

I tried to be casual as I mentioned to my husband the dream-presence of the young man standing in our room in the pre-dawn. Strange. I had not thought of him much as the years and the distance had widened between our lives. As always, when the young man came to mind, there was the twinge. Of having failed. Of having done it wrongly. Of deep regret.

Three months later an old college friend sat in my home, chatting over tea and bringing me up to date. *By the way, did you know that the young man dropped dead suddenly? It was this year. About three months ago, I believe.*

*

We are not so powerful or grandiose as to be responsible for the total outcomes in another individual's life. Our choices are ultimately our own, I suppose. But I cannot help wondering about the ways in which influence, rightly used today, impacts another person's journey to tomorrow.

Especially when God trusts you to bring a life to Him.

The young man. He was a gentle boy with a lion's heart. His view of God was born, shaped, then deformed by a girl who highjacked God's influence in his life. She kept it for herself. At his dying hour, it was not ultimately Claudette that he would need. It was her God.

And I never got to say, "I am sorry."

They say Jacob wrestled with an angel.

Or with God.

Or somebody.

And they say it wounded him in the hip

joint. Or the thigh.

Or something.

Kicked his butt, for sure. Umm-Hm.

Left him deformed for good. Hobbled.

With some kind of

bad limp, they say.

Yes sir, I knew that Jacob.

All's I know is this:

That some people walk straighter now,

limping,

Than they ever did with two good legs.

*

I am

So

Beautiful to me.

Chapter Ten

Scar Gazing

Scars are ugly.

They mar the landscape of skin.

Scars interrupt.

They remind us not to presume that life will always proceed as it began. Not as we had imagined.

Scars make us curious, but not curious enough.

I wonder about the bitter women whom I am forced to deal with because they are a part of my life. I too often curse their glaring, boisterous, emotional scars that have defiled so many ... myself included. And I forget to remember that I do not know the whole story.

Scars. Make us react. Sometimes we judge each other. Unless we care enough to come really close and touch the place, scars can lead us to conclusions that are, often, so wrong.

Scars make people turn away from us. And they cause us to turn away, and hide. They make us lonely, because of people's inability to look, and because of our shame at having them.

"Then Jesus said to Thomas, Put your finger

Here, and see my hands.

Put your hand into the

Wound in my side."

(John 20:27)

I have a precious sister-friend of almost 20 years. Pat bears scars on her face, on her jaw, on her neck. Far too long she stayed away. Stayed behind. Lurked in the shadows. She made herself uneasily comfortable on the periphery of risk and relationship. Since childhood, unkind people inflicted deep wounds on her heart simply because they were too shallow, too stupid or dull to discern the difference between a face and a life. Too few looked past the shallow public "standards" of what is beautiful or desirable, to know the woman of incredible passion, generosity and spiritual wealth.

My friend is a wounded woman, made strong because ... well, life demanded it. She lives most days of her life in excruciating, uncomplaining pain. She has suffered facial and throat tumors that with every extraction seem to reproduce themselves in a kind of malignant persistence. They have threatened to paralyze her speech, and even choke off her *air* ... *her very air* ... since she was a little girl. Who can imagine a child's terror when life is held teasingly before her, at every cycle? Pat has suffered through countless surgical procedures and reconstructions, only to end up at the same place of pain, again and again. She loves and serves a God who has not chosen thus far to manifest a healing change. People who have never learned to gaze upon scars with comprehending eyes have walked past this jewel of a human being and been the poorer for the passing. How she loves! How she cares for others! How she sees what most persons miss in the equations of the soul.

This same woman, in spite of pain and scars, opens her mouth and you can hear music that comes from another realm called *very heaven*. Vocal chords that have wrestled for the air to speak a word have paid life back with praise.

> *"Father if you be willing, remove this cup from me.*
> *Nevertheless not my will, but thine be done.*
> *Then there appeared an angel from heaven,*
> *Strengthening him."*
> *(Luke 22:42)*

Nevertheless.

Undeserved suffering and survival can compose music that arrests the ear of God and causes God to smile. Her music salves my heart and causes me to stop and weep and bend low in worshipful confrontation. Even angels come to visit.

"Yes, God *is* real."

From her wounds issue the healing melodies that only a person can know who has been crushed alive ... and has chosen to live ... *with the scars*.

Count Your Own

Each scar has a story behind it. The knee I skinned at five when I first learned to ride my bicycle. The chicken pock on my forehead that tormented me; when all the others healed it left a telltale crater. The snake scar on my back is the signature of the lung surgeon who saved my 14-year-old withering life. The anchor on my belly, a belly that offered itself to the experiments and hopes that might have produced babies. The "road" across my chest where a breast used to be, that scar that tried to make me stoop and be ashamed of my different-ness far too long. Scars. Go on, examine your own.

Scar tissue usually no longer has feeling. The nerve end-ings have been sacrificed. A trade-off for the silence. The scar is a place of deadening, of protection. It is place where the skin has been made ten times stronger at the point of the wound.

The thing that hurts about scar tissue is the attachments. If there is any pain at all, it's from the places (or persons) lying *just next* to the scar. Connections, where the scar demands liv-ing skin to stretch to accommodate it. Where it pulls. Where it itches and torments. Where it fussily keeps on showing off, getting bigger and bigger as a keloid. Or *adhesions*. I am told that adhesions are like angry, aggressive, already-been-chewed bubble-gum. Or perhaps a hungry spider's web ... attaching to and claiming whatever points it can. Adhesions hurt *inside* the body. Scar tissue you cannot see, but which won't let you forget. It is at the joining points, those bridges at which the microscopic announcements are, that get you. The verge of terrible remembering.

Pain around the scar. At instants it is pointed, sharp, jab-bing pain. But mostly the pain has dulled by time and read-justments. It whispers that even though I am somehow healed from what "was," there is the pathetic irony that I can still feel "what might have been." There remain tricky *attach-*

ments between the spots that are dead and those that are not. There are tiny caverns in the flesh or in the heart that are *not* scarred over. Scars live *right next door* to new hopes and dreams. They are forever bound in an unintentional dance. That is *life; in the midst of it there is an unwitting kinship* to what has been forever altered.

The memory of pain haunts my hope.

But hope refuses to die, in spite of the connection to pain. The adhesions.

In Another Time

Scars must be honored if the soul is to be enlarged.

They call us to an unashamed meditation.

Scars are the telltale signs of redemption. They announce, "Peace and rest, to the jagged edges of all that wrestled with my sanity and my survival."

Here we are.

Quieted in love.

Selah.

Yes, the Scars are Holy. They are sanctified inscriptions, when read well. "What once seemed unbearable has indeed been borne." Wounds that threaten to smother my very life at this instant will, one day soon, hurt no longer. At least not in this same hot, crushing, screaming way. Just look again at the *old* scars. They mount the holy pulpit of your search for meaning, and they proclaim aloud — humming and celebrating, strutting back and forth — that our weeping, oozing, bloody wounds *do* staunch. And by and by, they will begin to make sense in the light of God's eternal story.

Hallelujah to God's Name!

I gaze upon my scars and I listen. Again and again they chorus me: *We do get over the pain ... We do get over ... We do get over ... We do get over ... See?? We do get over!!*

Scar tissue. Maybe it is a physical parable on the rewards of surviving. You can still hurt about many things in many areas, but at least you will never have to experience *that* particular pain again. They proclaim to the world "that" did not kill her then. Nor, now, will *this*. For that reason alone, scars deserve not only to be tolerated. Not only to be remembered. Or just lived with.

Scars deserve to be Unveiled.

Contemplated with love.

In another time, in a new social future, perhaps we shall evolve. Then it shall be that after long absences and spells of aloneness, perhaps then we will not greet one another with handshakes or cheek-to-cheek touches. In another time, in a different future our customs may evolve. In *that* day we shall...

Greet.

Welcome.

Signal the immense value your life holds for me.

And mine for you.

But differently.

In another time of our imagining, reunions that matter will not warrant a cursory hug, or even a peck on the lips. Perhaps in another time, in a social context when we are not ashamed to love, and be blessed by love without conditions on it, I will greet you by honoring *the scar that I see*. Or you will honor me by unveiling *the one you have kept hidden*. Trusting me with it, knowing we will handle one another with tenderness. And because we shall be so deliriously happy for our mutual survival, we will gaze upon the scars. **Then kiss them for one another.** That shall be our holy greeting.

For, without words, we shall both know what it has cost us ... to simply be here.

With one another.

Once more.

Selah.

Until that time, kiss *your own* scars. And rejoice.

Again, I say *Rejoice!*

Visit us at
www.ClaudetteACopeland.org
or call
toll-free 1-866-637-6394

Stories From
INNER
s'pace
Confessions
Of A Preacher Woman and Other Tales